REVELATION

THE LETTERS TO THE SEVEN CHURCHES

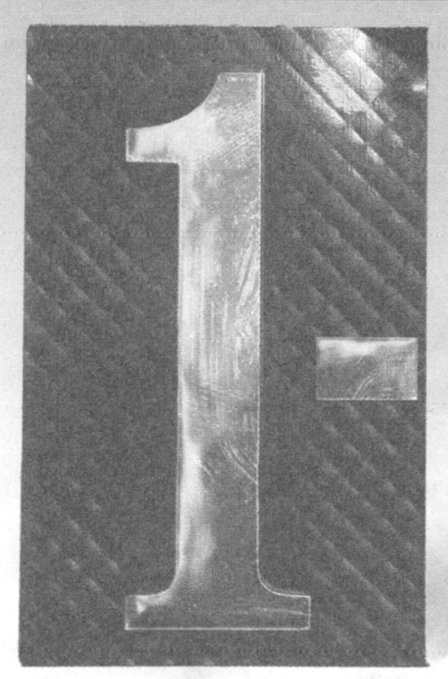

LifeWay Press®
Nashville, TN

ISBN: 978-1-4627-9489-8
Item: 005802003

Subject Area: Bible Studies
Dewey Decimal Classification Number: 228
Subject Heading: N.T. REVELATION-STUDY
Printed in the United States of America

LifeWay Christian Resources
One LifeWay Plaza
Nashville, TN 37234

We believe that the Bible has God for its author; salvation for its end; and truth, without any mixture of error, for its matter and that all Scripture is totally true and trustworthy. To review LifeWay's doctrinal guidelines, please visit www.lifeway.com/doctrinalguideline.

Cover Image, Title Page Image, Contents Page Image, and Chapter Beginnings Image: iStock Photos

CONTENTS

MEET THE SETTING, SCRIBE, AND SUBJECT OF REVELATION

The very first word of this remarkable book is *apocalupsis*. It literally means a disclosure or unveiling. It declares that what is contained in these pages is truth that had been hidden until that time. This unveiling was sent "to show his servants what must soon take place" (Rev. 1:1). This unveiling was for the church. It was for their building up and to provide understanding of what lay ahead.

The persecution addressed in this unveiling was likely that under Domitian in the years AD 81-95. It was preceded by 25 years of persecution under Nero, whose persecution had been more irregular. The persecution under Domitian was much more intense and constant.

At the time of the writing, about AD 95, "Caesar is Lord" was the required confession of the Roman Empire. The reigning Caesar was Domitian and he controlled the empire. He demanded to be worshiped as the lord of the earth. Early believers refused to declare that Caesar was lord. After all, the great confession of their young faith was "Jesus is Lord." Severe persecution erupted at their refusal to bow before Caesar. Hounding, ridicule, exile, and death were their lot. It was into that world of hatred and hostility that the Book of Revelation was delivered.

The greatest danger, however, was not physical. The most sinister and dangerous of all persecution was the heresy and its attendant evils. These things were deeply entwined in the cultural landscape of the first-century church through false teachers.

John the beloved apostle and pastor of the church in Ephesus wrote Revelation while exiled to the Isle of Patmos, which lay in the Aegean Sea about 45 miles from Ephesus. John was the son of Zebedee and Salome, and brother of James. Zebedee had been a fishermen successful enough to have hired workers to assist in the business (Mark 1:20). John and James were fisherman on the Sea of Galilee in partnership with Simon Peter (Luke 5:10). They were among the first disciples to leave all to follow Jesus Christ in their youth. These brothers were known for their quick temper and aggressive nature, being labeled by Jesus as "Sons of Thunder" (Mark 3:17) when they wanted to call down fire from heaven upon a Samaritan village that refused to receive Jesus and the disciples (Luke 9:52-54).

At one point in their companionship with Jesus, the brothers asked to have the honor of sitting on His right and left hand with Him in His glory (Mark 10:37). This request was met with a rebuke from Jesus. They were marked with both quick temper and desire for prominence.

John never lacked for courage to testify about the resurrected Lord. When he and Peter were confronted by Jewish leaders for preaching the gospel (Acts 4:5-7) they were described as "uneducated and untrained men" (v. 13). When commanded not to preach or teach in Jesus' name, Peter and John courageously replied, "Whether it's right in the sight of God for us to listen to you rather than to God, you decide; for we are unable to stop speaking about what we have seen and heard" (vv. 19-20). Now, as he penned this prophecy, John was the much-beloved, greatly mellowed patriarch, who served as pastor of the church in Ephesus.

John opened this remarkable book by declaring, "The revelation of Jesus Christ that God gave him to show his servants what must soon take place" (Rev. 1:1). From beginning to end, this is a book about the Lord Jesus Christ. It is a "testimony of Jesus Christ" (v. 2). Additionally, it contains an incomparable promise: "Blessed is the one who reads aloud the words of this prophecy, and blessed are those who hear the words of this prophecy and keep what is written in it, because the time is near" (v. 3). This promised blessing requires careful study to absorb this prophecy into our hearts. Such a study will be richly rewarding.

Immediately "the seven churches in Asia" (v. 4) are identified as the recipients of this prophecy. Jesus Christ is described as "the one who is, who was, and who is to come ... the faithful witness, the firstborn from the dead and the ruler of the kings of the earth" (vv. 4-5).

This book is about the ultimate triumph of the Lord Jesus Christ over all evil. "Look, he is coming with the clouds, and every eye will see him, even those who pierced him. And all the tribes of the earth will mourn over him. So it is to be. Amen. 'I am the Alpha and the Omega,' says the Lord God, 'the one who is, who was, and who is to come, the Almighty'" (vv. 7-8).

The synopsis of the book is found in 1:19: "Therefore write what you have seen, what is, and what will take place after this." While the book occasionally looks on past events, the basic focus is on the future.

Revelation is filled with intriguing and significant symbols. As a teenage boy I was fascinated by the "beast coming up out of the sea" (13:1) and the "beast coming up out of the earth" (v. 11). Then, there was the challenge to understand the number of the beast—666. Symbols in pictorial language and specific numbers, in challenging complexity, are numerous throughout these chapters.

In Revelation, we get a unique view of the inner workings of the Godhead. The first chapter speaks of "Jesus," "God," and "the Spirit." This first chapter also gives us the goal and the conclusion of the book. Revelation begins with Jesus Christ and ends with His triumphant return. It is written in the midst of unbridled persecution and ends with the establishment of His kingdom on earth, accompanied with believers of all ages who participate in the operation of His kingdom.

This prophecy has been received with awe, frustration, and skepticism over the centuries. It is one of the most difficult books of prophecy in Scripture. Some assert that Revelation deals predominantly with first-century events, including the destruction of Jerusalem in AD 70.

Others see it as a wide sweep of history from John's time until the second coming of Christ. They see it as a summary of the great periods or dispensations in the history of Christianity.

Below: Modern-day port of Patmos from the entrance to the cave of the Apocalypse.

ILLUSTRATOR PHOTO/ BOB SCHATZ (28/1/11)

Still others interpret the book as primarily symbols and allegories, not literal events, showing the ongoing battle between good and evil and pointing to the certain success of God's redemptive purposes and the establishment of His everlasting kingdom.

The view of this writer is that after the letters to the seven churches, the Revelation deals predominantly with the end times of our world. It is an undeniable word from God that sees the world coming to its divinely ordained conclusion in the victorious return of the Lord Jesus Christ and an eternity of peace for all of His people.

The future events described are vital and necessary. Our faith embraces the biblical expectation—indeed necessity—of the literal, bodily, visible return of the Lord Jesus Christ. God's faithfulness demands the climactic events described in this book.

The theme of this significant prophecy is the glory of the Lord Jesus Christ. This is the capstone of all Christology. It shows us that history is His story and He will bring this world to the conclusion of His choosing. It is in His hands and our part is to be ready. Jesus is the pre-existent and divine Son of God. He is our great High Priest who offered Himself upon the altar of God at the cross—He is the Lamb of God who brings forgiveness of sins and salvation to all who believe.

Revelation describes the Jesus of history who was crucified in Jerusalem as the sacrifice for our sins. He rose from the dead and ascended into heaven and will return as King of kings and Lord of lords. The drama unfolding is seen in two dimensions—heaven and earth. The obvious reason is that it is God's plan to have His will done on earth as it is done in heaven, as Jesus reminded us in teaching us to pray, "Your kingdom come. Your will be done on earth as it is in heaven" (Matt. 6:10-11). The culmination of the ages and the reality of His kingdom on earth will happen regardless of the intense opposition of Satan and evil forces described in Revelation.

Jesus will return as promised at His ascension: "This same Jesus, who has been taken from you into heaven, will come in the same way that you have seen him going into heaven" (Acts 1:11). Jesus Himself declared, "the sign of the Son of Man will appear in the sky, and then all the peoples of the earth will mourn; and they will see the Son of Man coming on the clouds of heaven with power and great glory" (Matt. 24:30).

> Revelation demonstrates the unity of the Bible. There are 404 verses in this book and 285 direct quotations out of the Old Testament. There are over 550 references to the Old Testament. In contrast the Book of Matthew has only 92 references to the Old Testament; and the Book of Hebrews, considered to be the most Jewish of all New Testament books, has only 102 references to the Old Testament. Revelation, like

no other New Testament book, has a distinctive Old Testament flavor.[1]

And like no other book, Revelation points to the unity of both Old and New Testaments. In the pages of Revelation, it is as though God has brought all the threads of prophecy that run throughout Scripture and woven them into a beautiful tapestry for us to see. Revelation shows us that there is no power in heaven, on earth, or in hell itself that can cancel the plans of God. Herein is the bold declaration of the inevitability and invincibility of the purposes of God.

The crowning joy of heaven will be to see the face of our beloved Savior and Lord. The climax of God's creation will be the new Jerusalem. The climax of eternity will be coming face to face with Him, forever reigning, ruling, and living with Him.

1. James T. Draper, *The Unveiling*, (Nashville: Broadman Press, 1984) 12.

THE MAJESTIC GLORY OF FATHER AND SON

REVELATION 1:1-20

Sitting like a partially completed jigsaw puzzle in the midst of twelve islands, the island of Patmos is the setting for the Book of Revelation. It is a scraggly island of only 24 square miles with mountain peaks rising quickly, its highest peak nearly 900 feet above sea level. The island is 10 miles long and its widest spot is 6 miles. It has an extremely jagged coastline with some spots being less than a mile across. The island reveals sparse vegetation and rocky landscapes, yet it is one of the most beautiful settings in the Aegean Sea. Resting boldly in the scenic waters of the sea, it is 45 miles west of Miletus and Ephesus in Asia Minor.

A temple to the Greek goddess Artemis (Roman goddess Diana) was built on the island in the 4th century BC. Patmos became one of a number of islands used to exile accused criminals.

John the apostle was exiled there about AD 95 by the Roman Emperor Domitian. John's crime? Proclaiming the gospel of Jesus Christ! It is not known whether John was exiled to live there or placed there to work in the mines. Soon after Domitian's death, he was allowed to return to his beloved Ephesus for the remainder of his life.

The island was replete with inlets and harbors around its 25-30 mile circumference with most of the island falling abruptly into the sea. It boasted of magnificent scenery with its rocky crags resting in the clear blue waters of the Aegean.

It was while there that John received the prophecy found in the Book of Revelation. This prophecy deals with two places—heaven and earth. It deals with two times—now and the future. It points to one inevitable, climactic event—the second coming of the Lord Jesus Christ to establish His kingdom on earth.

The time of the writing was in a period of excessive cruelty and vicious carnage. This persecution is likely that which occurred under Domitian, AD 81-96, which was preceded by 25 years of violent tyranny under Nero. Under Nero the attacks were sporadic, but under Domitian they were more intense and orchestrated.

Living in a Hostile Culture

John lived and wrote during a time when there was great hostility toward believers and the gospel message—even to the point of physical persecution.

List some examples of ways that our culture today is hostile toward the gospel message.

1.

2.

3.

Commit to pray God's protection for those believers around the world who are suffering for their faith today.

Against that fierce backdrop this prophecy anticipates the day when the Lord Jesus Christ will return and bring His kingdom into literal reality, in a real place and among real people. The coming Day of the Lord will be the birth pains of the golden age of God's eternal kingdom. Everything in this universe will be destroyed and a new world will emerge. That was the living hope of the people of God in the time John wrote this prophecy.

John called this **the revelation of Jesus Christ that God gave him to show his servants what must soon take place** because **the time is near**. The expectation of the imminent return of Jesus Christ has always dominated the hope of believers. When the return of Christ is relegated to some distant future, we rob our faith of its vitality and our witness of its urgency. It is the anticipation of the soon return of Jesus Christ that creates passion and urgency within believers.

This opening chapter is all about the majestic glory of God and the Son of God. Divine authority shines dominantly throughout the entire book. The Godhead is clearly seen as God the Father, God the Son, and God the Holy Spirit. This revelation of Jesus Christ given by God the Father through an **angel** to John is called **the word of God** and is **the testimony of Jesus Christ**.

The prophecy confirms the certainty of our returning Lord. Great blessing is promised to those who hear or read **this prophecy**. The opening words, designating **the seven churches in Asia** as the recipients, contains a remarkable promise of **grace and peace** as the gift of the Lord Himself. Grace brings undeserved gifts from God. Peace is the result of grace.

The first verses present a unique description of the working of the Trinity. Jesus Christ and God are introduced in the first two verses. It is **the revelation of Jesus Christ that God gave him to show his servants what must soon take place. He made it known by sending his angel to his servant John, who testified to the word of God and to the testimony of Jesus Christ, whatever he saw**.

Jesus Christ, the Son of God, is the dominant Person of the entire prophecy. Although John never used the title "Holy Spirit" in Revelation, his reference to the **seven spirits before his throne** (or "the seven-fold Spirit," understood by many Bible students to mean the Holy Spirit) and his frequent mention of the "Spirit" confirm that he is referring to the Holy Spirit.

Jesus Christ is described in three specific ways: **the faithful witness, the firstborn from the dead and the ruler of the kings of the earth**. As the **faithful witness,** He is the One who is absolutely certain to tell the truth. The **firstborn from the dead** speaks of His resurrection. **Firstborn** indicates that there are more to follow, which speaks of our resurrection. As the **ruler of the kings of the earth**, it is clear that all earthly authorities are allowed by Him and can continue their rule only with His approval. He is our Sovereign Lord!

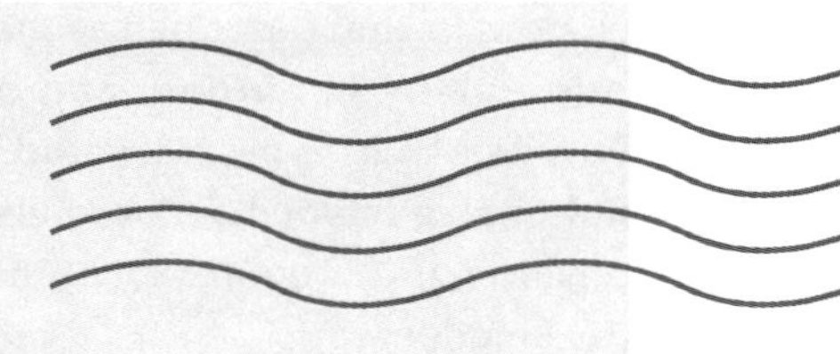

We Know How It Ends!

Have you ever read a novel or watched a movie for a second time? If so, you already know the ending as the story unfolded that second time. In the very first chapter of Revelation, John told us how it will end! Read Revelation 1:7-8.

How can knowing that Christ conquers all in the end help you as you face challenges this coming week ...
At home?

At work?

At church?

In your neighborhood?

He is further described as the One **who loves us and has set us free from our sins by his blood, and made us a kingdom, priests to his God and Father—to him be glory and dominion forever and ever. Amen**. Saints are not only redeemed and forgiven—**set ... free from our sins**—but given great position and prominence in the kingdom. There are no insignificant people in His kingdom.

Revelation reveals that from the crushing violence, turmoil, and bloodshed, exceeding anything that this earth has ever seen, will emerge the kingdom age where all evil, hostility, and slaughter will be judged and destroyed by God Himself.

At the very beginning of Revelation, John told us how it will all end (vv. 7-8). He could not wait to tell that the Lord Jesus Christ conquers and establishes His kingdom. He did not tease readers by holding and concealing the ultimate result until the end. What is coming is so spectacular that he was compelled to declare, **Look, he is coming with the clouds, and every eye will see him**. No doubt about the outcome. No one will miss seeing His visible return. His kingdom will be everlasting (v. 8). This echoes the apostle Paul's description of Him as "the King eternal, immortal, invisible, the only God, [to whom] be honor and glory forever and ever. Amen" (1 Tim. 1:17).

God is pictured as the One who is above time, **the Alpha and the Omega ... the one who is, who was, and who is to come, the Almighty**. Past, present, and future are seen at the same time by God. That's why He can record our lives before we were ever born (Ps. 139:16).

He possesses all wisdom and knowledge. Alpha and omega are the first and last letters of the Greek alphabet. Everything able to be described in human words are perfectly known by God.

John described himself as **your brother and partner in the affliction** (Rev. 1:9). He was living through the devastation they all were experiencing.

John explained that he was on **Patmos**, but **in the Spirit on the Lord's Day**. This statement describes all believers in every age. We are in the world but not of the world. We must function in this present world, but our eternal home is in heaven. In Colossians 1:2 Paul described himself as "in Christ at Colossae." That is the crucial dynamic of the Christian life. In Christ, yet in the world.

Jesus then instructed John to **send [the scroll] to the seven churches: Ephesus, Smyrna, Pergamum, Thyatira, Sardis, Philadelphia, and Laodicea** (Rev. 1:11). Describing Himself as **the First and the Last, and the Living One**, He knows the beginning and the end and all in between. He is the final source of wisdom and truth. He is the Almighty God!

We observe a phenomenal picture of the true spirit of worship: **When I saw him, I fell at his feet like a dead man**. This is a compelling illustration of the spirit of genuine worship. **I heard ... I turned ... I saw ... I fell at his feet**.

Whenever we are confronted with the Lord, our response must always be that of complete awe and reverence.

Jesus laid His right hand on John and said: **Don't be afraid. I am the First and the Last, and the Living One. I was dead, but look—I am alive forever and ever, and I hold the keys of death and Hades.**

The **seven stars** just seen in His hand are the angels, or pastors, of the seven churches. If the Lord holds the pastors of the churches in His hands, surely we can hold them in our hearts! The pastors hold a unique place in God's redemptive purposes. The **lampstands** represent the seven churches. Here is an incomparable picture of our Lord and our response to Him.

Now see the key verse in this chapter: **Write what you have seen, what is, and what will take place after this**. **What you have seen, what is** refers to chapters 2–3. **What will take place after this** is found in chapters 4–22. Revelation reveals the fulfillment of God's purposes when the Lord will return!

The Letters to the Seven Churches

These letters were prepared for seven real churches in a real place—Asia Minor. "The seven cities mentioned form an irregular circle, and are listed in the order in which a messenger might visit them if commissioned to deliver the letters."[1] The time is near the end of the first century AD. These churches had been infiltrated by immoral practices, heresy, and all kinds of evil. These characteristics and qualities have been present in all churches throughout history.

EPHESUS was the largest city in the Roman Province of Asia. It was the commercial and political hub of the province. Located south of the Temple of Artemis (the Artemision) between Mt. Pion and Mt. Koressos, it was an ancient city and goes back into the second millennium before Christ.

Situated on the main highway that tied the Aegean Sea with the rich trade routes in the east, it was the major commercial city in Asia Minor. Paul first came into the city on his second missionary journey and settled there for at least two years on his third missionary journey. The seven churches of Revelation 2–3 came into existence through Paul's ministry in Ephesus.

Ephesus was located about 35 miles southeast of Smyrna and about 40 miles north of Miletus. The Cayster river flowed through Ephesus and the silt from the river gradually caused the city to be several miles up the river in the first century. It still had access to the Aegean Sea by the Çayster River, and had an adequate harbor on the river.

Ephesus was important in every way, politically, economically, and religiously. It was the *de facto* capital for the Roman province of Asia (though Pergamum was the official capital). It was a "free" city, which made it self-governing and exempt from having Roman soldiers stationed there. It was also an "assize" city which meant that it was a place where Roman justice was administered.

It had a major banking presence and the primary worship of Artemis was there. The massive marble temple of Artemis was one of the seven wonders of the ancient world. It was built on a foundation 420 feet long and 240 feet wide and named for the Greek goddess Artemis. In later days the Romans named her Diana. The massive roof was supported by 127 pillars of Parian marble, each 60 feet tall, sculptured with mythological scenes, some overlaid with gold. Sitting a mile northeast of the city just beneath a high hill, it was the first thing seen when ships entered the harbor.

The temple itself had the right of asylum for individuals accused of crimes. This area extended various distances around the edifice at different times, and for a period was extended to include parts of the city itself. All kinds of fugitives poured into Ephesus.

The streets were lined with many significant buildings. There was a town council chamber, a town hall, an imperial temple dedicated to Augustus, along with many temples and places of business. The massive amphitheater seated 24,000 people.

At this time the city's population of 250,000 was probably the fourth largest in the world. It was from Ephesus that John was exiled to the offshore island of Patmos. The church in Ephesus was an active church, but had abandoned its passion and love for Christ.

SMYRNA was a strong commercial city located 35 miles northwest of Ephesus. It was one of the most beautiful cities in the ancient world, called "The Glory of Asia" or "The Crown of Asia." It had impressive paved streets lined with many temples. A public theater which claimed to be one of the largest in Asia, a famous stadium that held annual athletic games, and a magnificent library joined the temples along the way. Smyrna was known for its loyalty to Rome dating back to around 195 BC. Its population during New Testament times was between 100,000 and 200,000.

It had a landlocked and protected harbor. The city rose to the top of mount Pagus, some 600 feet above the inland harbor, as the eloquent, dynamic buildings and temples wrapped around its summit. The most famous street was the

Street of Gold, which ran diagonally just below the apex of Mount Pagus. The distinctive buildings at the top gave the appearance of a crown on the city. The Street of Gold ran like a necklace just below the crown of the city.

A large and influential number of Jews lived in Smyrna. They made life miserable for believers and led the attack on Polycarp, famous early Christian martyr, when he was executed there in AD 155.

PERGAMUM lay on a high hill just 16 miles from the coast. The city rose 1000 feet above the plains around the river Caicus. It was the city often credited with inventing and producing the parchment widely used in ancient days. It had been the capital city of the Attalid kingdom from 231-133 BC and was the capital of the Roman Province of Asia. The city contained many pagan centers, the most famous of which was dedicated to Asclepius, the god of medicine. The identifier of this god was a serpent wrapped around a pole, which became the symbol of the medical profession. Eumenes II built a massive altar to Zeus measuring 120 feet by 112 feet and resting on an 18-foot-high platform.

Pergamum expressed its loyalty to Rome with a temple for Caesar worship—the first such temple in Asia—which was mandatory for every Roman citizen. Each citizen received a certificate each year after offering worship to Caesar. It was obviously not a friendly place for Christians.

THYATIRA lay about 50 miles from the sea and was once a great military city. It was located 35 miles southeast of Pergamum. It was the smallest and least important of the seven cities. It emerged as a military outpost in 290 BC. It was the gateway to Pergamum with no natural defense, so was destined to be attacked, captured, destroyed, and rebuilt.

The main god was Tyrimnas, seen as a warrior welding a large two-headed axe. It was well known for the development of trade guilds, to one of which Lydia (Acts 16:14) may have belonged. The trade guilds consisted of clothiers, metal smiths, and others. The social activities of the guilds were attached to the worship of heathen gods. They became so popular and powerful that they took on political and religious importance.

SARDIS was about 30 miles southeast of Thyatira and was the chief city of the Hermus Valley, the most important of the major valleys. It was one of the most historic cities in Asia Minor, once capital of Lydia, home of the immensely wealthy King Croesus. The first coins to be minted of silver and gold were produced in Sardis.

The reputation of the city was tarnished by compromise and failure. It was considered impregnable because of its strong citadel, but was conquered twice by enemies because of the carelessness of its sentries regarding approaching enemies.

Sardis had become a name of contempt and a byword for decadent living, becoming the most notorious city of Asia Minor. It perhaps was more like a den of thieves than a civilized town.

PHILADELPHIA, situated 28 miles southeast of Sardis, was founded by Attalus, king of Pergamum, to become a center of Greek civilization. It was designed to spread the philosophy and language of Greece. Its purpose was to promote unity of customs, language, and loyalty to Greece. It was remarkably successful. By AD 19 Greek was the only language in the country.

Located on the Cogamis River, it was an area subject to volcanic eruptions and earthquakes. The most notable earthquake was in AD 17, which devastated the city. It was the epicenter of the earthquake, and aftershock tremors were felt for twenty years.

Few people actually lived in the city itself. Most spent their lives as farmers in the country. The city was undesirable because of the earthquakes and volcanic eruptions. But volcanic soil is extremely inviting for crops, especially grapes.

LAODICEA, 43 miles southeast of Philadelphia, was the key city in the wealthy province of Phrygia. Located in the narrow valley on the Lycus River at the strategic center of the Meander River Valley, it lay on a major trade route 99 miles from Ephesus. It was a fashionable city that was twice devastated by disaster and recovered without the aid of Rome.

Laodicean bankers were famous even in Rome. They were known for integrity in business, never diluting or cheapening the gold they used. The city boasted of its medical school and for producing a special eye ointment.

It was a very wealthy city of luxury and extravagance. It was also a place for Roman justice to be administered, and legal determinations made there were official Roman judgments.

An 8,000-foot mountain bordered the city on the south, and the mountains to the north, beyond Hierapolis, were topped with a white mineral formation that made it look like snow. Previously known as Diospolis and Rhodes, it was renamed around 261 BC by Antiochus II for his first wife Laodice.

Laodicea had such a large and powerful Jewish population that they were given freedom by Rome to observe the Sabbath and other Jewish rituals.

The seven letters were written to literal, historical churches. The churches were in near proximity, with the furthest distance between them being just over 100 miles. Some needed to be rebuked. Some needed to be encouraged. Each letter contained a word to the overcomer.

Many see these seven letters as representing various stages of the church historically. Some even conclude that the seven churches represent seven kinds of believers, both those who are true and those who are false. The conditions in these churches are always present in churches in all ages.

A CLOSER LOOK

Asia Minor

Asia Minor was first identified by that name around AD 400 by Christian historian Orosius. That designation was given for the region evangelized by the apostle Paul. It was the southwest part of Asia comprising most of modern Turkey. It was the link between the continent of Europe with the Near East.

Surrounded by high mountain ranges, its narrow passes connected the interior with the Near East. Deep channels brought numerous navigable rivers to the Aegean Sea.

Two of the seven wonders of the ancient world were found in Asia Minor: the Temple of Artemis (Diana) in Ephesus and the Tomb of Mausolus at Halicarnassus in Caria.

It was the home of the first western philosopher, Thales, from Miletus. Herodotus, famous Jewish historian known as the Father of History, was from Halicarnassus. The great philosopher and mathematician Pythagoras was born in Asia Minor as was the apostle Paul who was born in Tarsus.

The first coins used in trade were minted there. Under Roman rule Asia Minor was stabilized with roads and infrastructure being built. Coastal cities flourished with great prosperity.

Personal Reflection

1. Revelation 1:3 gives two blessings associated with the prophecy of the book, and a brief explanation for them. Based on your pattern of relating to this final book of the Bible, to what degree do you qualify for the blessings listed? Explain.

2. Review the descriptions of God the Father and God the Son in Revelation 1 and the explanations present in this chapter. Which stands out as most meaningful to you at this time? Why?

3. As we launch into this study of the seven churches of Revelation, what benefit do you expect to obtain?

1. John Stott, *What Christ Thinks of the Church* (London: Angus Hudson Ltd., 1990) 7.

EPHESUS

REVELATION 2:1-7

The significant city of Ephesus was the location for the first of the seven letters. The city itself was the most powerful city in every way in all of Asia Minor. The focus of the city was on the worship of Artemis that took place in a magnificent temple, one of the seven wonders of the ancient world. It was known as the Artemision. The ancient temple was destroyed in the 7th century BC and reconstructed around 540 BC. Destroyed by fire in 356 BC, it was again rebuilt over a number of years, 120 according to Roman historian Pliny.

The worship of Artemis involved very exotic rituals. Hundreds of eunuch priests, zealous priestesses and religious prostitutes served her. Ephesus was the world center for Artemis worship and was responsible for maintaining the cult's adherence to the tenets of the worship.

These rituals brought great wealth to the citizens of Ephesus because the temple became the world's largest bank during that time. People came from all over the world to worship and celebrate Artemis during exotic and erotic festivals. Huge processions honored her statues. Celebrations involved music, dancing, singing, and dramatic performances along with chanting of allegiance.

Two statues of Artemis were found in the Prytaneion, which was the seat of Greek government in Ephesus. It was comparable to our city hall. These indicate that the worship of Artemis controlled life in the city. The promise of long life, fertility, sexual fulfillment, and the seductive sexuality of the worship rituals shaped the culture of Ephesus. There were also many other pagan temples there.

Into that seductive culture the church at Ephesus was planted. Believers faced opposition from every side. The purity demanded of believers was directly contrary to the spirit of Ephesus. All trades were deeply entangled in the items and

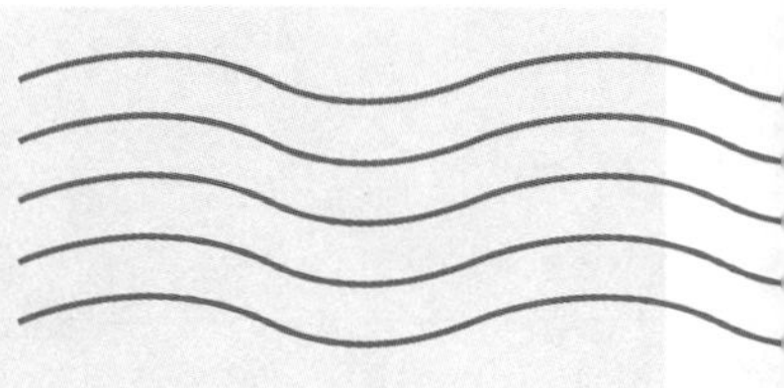

Seductive Culture

Worship of the pagan goddess Artemis dominated life in ancient Ephesus.

"The promise of long life, fertility, sexual fulfillment, and the seductive sexuality of the worship rituals shaped the culture of Ephesus. ... Into that seductive culture the church at Ephesus was planted."

Yet despite these pagan influences that spread into every area of their lives, the church in Ephesus thrived. In our culture today, pagan influences abound.

In what ways are we surrounded by a "seductive culture" today?

What are the traps or dangers of a seductive culture?

articles needed in the worship of Artemis, making it difficult for believers to secure the funds necessary for physical survival without denying their faith.

With the overwhelming number of people focused on false worship, believers were the objects of ridicule and hostility. In spite of the licentious atmosphere around them, the church in Ephesus thrived. It had an active and effective ministry. It was, undoubtedly, the most important church in all of Asia Minor.

The letter is addressed to the **angel** of the church. That word usually represented human messengers in Greek culture, rather than spirit messengers.

Above: The Library of Celsus and the south entrance gate to the agora.

ILLUSTRATOR PHOTO/ BOB SCHATZ (11/37/6)

It appears to address the messenger or pastor of the church. If actual angels were the ones to receive this message, it seems likely that God would have spoken directly to them and not have a man do it.

The Lord Jesus introduced Himself to the Ephesian church as **the one who holds the seven stars in his right hand and who walks among the seven golden lampstands**. Previously John explained that "The seven stars are the angels of the seven churches, and the seven lampstands are the seven churches" (Rev. 1:20).

In the Greek language the tense of verbs did not indicate time of action, but rather kind of action. Present tense indicated continual action, not just present action. What we would call past tense in Greek did not just speak of past action, but specific action at a point in past time that was still in force. The verbs *holds* and *walks* are both present active participles, indicating that these acts of the Lord Jesus Christ are constant. Our Lord holds the pastors of today's churches in His right hand and walks among the churches. He is always with His pastors and saints in the churches.

The Dedicated Ministry of the Church (Rev. 2:2-3)

The church in Ephesus was doing its job. Real ministry was taking place. It was a busy church that was theologically, morally, and ethically sound. The compliments our Lord gave to the church are remarkable.

The church had admirable **works**. Actual service was being accomplished and lives were being touched. Energetic and physically exhausting **labor** was being expended. The apparent ministry of the church was impressive. The **endurance** of the church was exceptional. These believers faced all opposition without flinching and never slacked off on their task.

It did not tolerate evil. This church tested those who claimed to be **apostles** and proved they were liars. Because such testing is always an unpleasant and tedious pursuit, this compliment is even more commendable.

They were a church with the gift of discernment. They had encountered false teachers and did not **tolerate evil people**. The church was careful to keep all evil doctrines out of its fellowship. Having proven the false teachers to be liars, they stood tall in the face of tremendous opposition.

We see this further as they responded to the teaching of the Nicolaitans (see v. 6) and hated that heresy. They were discriminating. Their doctrinal strength and beliefs were without blemish. As John had instructed in 1 John 4:1, they had tested the spirits to determine if they were from God. They meticulously searched the Scripture to compare what the Nicolaitans were teaching against the apostolic message they had received. This was a church strong in its doctrinal convictions.

Evidently they had faced strong opposition in the city. The Lord spoke of their perseverance under many hardships for His sake. Many religious temples dotted the landscape. Some of the citizens practiced the magical acts from the East. The city was consumed with the worship of Artemis, the dominant god of Asia.

Believers were an oddity to the bulk of the people and greatly maligned. Jesus said, **I know that you have persevered and endured hardships for the sake of my name, and have not grown weary**. They remained rock solid in the face of extreme pressure and had not denied Christ. In spite of all the opposition they had persevered and had demonstrated a great reserve of strength. They did not grow weary even in the face of intense attacks.

This is not the pastor's opinion of the church. It was not from the chamber of commerce of Ephesus. It was not a deacon or committee consensus. Jesus, the One who walks among the churches, who understands and knows the true condition of the church, was the One speaking. He said it was a working church, a laboring church, and a patient church. Persistent in their faithfulness and untiring in their service, the Lord commended them.

From our Lord's description of the church in Ephesus, what could possibly be wrong? The penetrating eye of our Lord Jesus Christ saw what no human eye could observe. He, alone, detected the fatal failure of the church.

The Destructive Spirit in the Church (Rev. 2:4)

In one simple sentence, the picture of the church radically changed. The Lord declared that one large debit canceled out all their credit. The church seemed to be doing everything right, but for the wrong reason. They stood for God in an ungodly way. They had lost themselves in the outward mechanics of service to the Lord, but had **abandoned** their first love and passion for Him. They had lost the intensity of their first love. They forgot why they were doing what they were doing. That defies analysis. There is simply no way to adequately describe this.

Perhaps they now loved the praise of men more than they desired the praise of God. Maybe it was that they were seeking prestige or position, or it could be that it was just the right thing to do in the culture of Ephesus. If our worship and service for God is not saturated with a passion for the Lord Jesus, then our service has no lasting value.

Some express concern about whether **the love you had at first** refers to love of fellow believers or love for God. But it stands to reason that both would be indicated. When we discard our first love for Christ, we will not long continue to love others.

First love is focused, attentive, impassioned, and exuberant. It is incandescent and blazes in intensity. When you genuinely love someone, everything in your life is affected by it. Loving Christ must be foundational to our mission. It is not our energy or creativity that blesses the world, nor our rituals and ceremonies that help others. It is not our orthodox theology that uplifts the world. It is our love for Christ and for each other that makes the difference.

See how subtle this failure was in Ephesus. When Paul wrote to the church at Thessalonica, he described their "work produced by faith, your labor motivated by love, and your endurance inspired by hope in our Lord Jesus Christ" (1 Thess. 1:3). When Jesus spoke of the Ephesian church He simply spoke of **your works, your labor, and your endurance**. He omitted the words "produced by faith," "motivated by love," and "inspired by hope" that characterized the Thessalonians. It was just **works ... labor ... endurance.**

Without love works might continue, labor could increase, and endurance might hang on, but without hope. How subtle and deceptive is the loss of first love!

The Ephesians deliberately **abandoned** their first love and fervor that they had for the Lord Jesus. They yielded to the ever-present temptation to devote their attention to sound doctrine and vigorous activities, rather than to their relationship with the Lord. In the process, they discarded their love for Christ. Without continuous and zealous love for Christ, everything we do as a church means nothing.

The Demanding Response Required (Rev. 2:5-7a)

Jesus described the Ephesian believers as **fallen**. At first glance, this does not sound like a fallen church. On the surface it looked like a very efficient and responsible church. But their service had become routine, impersonal, and ritualistic. Their worship was conventional and habitual. The old fire from above was gone.

The enemy of the church is formalism, getting into a habit of doing the ministry of the church without passion. Doing things for God had taken the place of a fiery love for Christ. Worship is like a telescope. It is not something to look at, but something to look through. The Ephesians had reversed that, and their first love for the Lord had disappeared. It is amazing how much work can be done without love and even without the Holy Spirit.

God forbid that we should ever do what we do without love for Him and without His presence and power. This fallen church had done so deliberately, as indicated by the word **abandoned**. They made a rational decision to continue to go through the motions of faithfulness without the love for the Savior by which the church was born.

Jesus gave three commands in verse 5 to guide the church to a restoration of first love.

1. **Remember** is a present imperative verb which demands ongoing and regular action. We are to remember, and keep on remembering, how it was when we first became a Christ follower. The excitement and thrill of newfound faith must be guarded by remembering. How soon we get used to being saved! How soon we remove the Lord from His place in our lives. We can recapture our first love, but it begins with continually remembering the grace of God that brought us from death to life, from darkness to light.

2. **Repent** is an aorist imperative verb, meaning that this is a command and not a suggestion. The aorist tense speaks of something that happened at a specific time in the past and stands today as having been done. It refers to a godly sorrow for our sins and a sharp break with evil. To repent of abandoning our first love, and focusing again on Him and what He has done for us, is required if we

are to recapture that first passion. Judgment is revocable if we repent. Twice in this verse Jesus called the church to repent. Without repentance the fervency of our first love cannot be rekindled.

Jesus said that if the Ephesian church did not recapture their first love, He would **remove your lampstand** and reject the church. Without real love for Jesus Christ, the reason for the church to exist vanishes. A church without love for Jesus is useless.

3. **Do the works you did at first.** This, too, is an aorist imperative verb which takes us back to the time of our conversion. When we first came to Christ, we confessed our sins to Him. We wanted Him to be Lord of our lives. We repented of our sin. Jesus demands that we do it again! Repent and return to Him is His command!

What a severe cost we pay when we abandon our first love. There is misery in our hearts, but there is also unspeakable grief that we have hurt the One we really love the most. But we do not have to remain without that first love. Remember, repent, and return to Him. Love Him like we did when we first became a Christ follower.

At Ephesus, the loss of first love was a deliberate choice believers made. The word used to describe that choice was *abandoned*. It was not a casual choice. It was not drifting into indifference. It was a specific, deliberate act of placing something else in the place of love for Christ.

The Lord next revealed the consequences of refusing to return to the first love of the church. If they did not remember, repent, and do the works they did at the first, then, **I will come to you and remove your lampstand from its place, unless you repent.** John Phillips put it this way, "No love, no light is the rule. Love is to be paramount: nothing less will do. If there is no real love for the Lord Jesus, the reason for the assembly's existence has vanished.... It gives the wrong impression of what Christianity is all about, and it is best removed."[1]

Once again the question of false teachers appears. The Lord complimented the church since they **hate the practices of the Nicolaitans, which I also hate**. It is important for us to note that they did not hate the people who followed the heresy of the Nicolaitans; rather they hated their actions and beliefs—"the practices." Certainly, we are called to oppose and despise heresy, but never the heretic. He is an object of God's love and a person in need of redemption. The Lord commended them for hating what He hates.

Little is known of the origin of the doctrine of the Nicolaitans. Some say that it comes from Nicolaus who was chosen as one of seven deacons in Acts 6. Christian tradition says that he became an apostate and adopted a form of Gnosticism. Other believe that the Nicolaitans were part of Gnosticism, but not from Nicolaus. Still others place the origin of the Nicolaitans on followers of Balaam or Jezebel from the Old Testament, or perhaps from both of them.

Wherever it came from, it was a developed theology strong enough to be established at Ephesus and Pergamum. It clearly was outside the boundaries of biblical theology. It is likely that this heresy taught that believers were free from all law and could live as they pleased. It was a perversion of the clear teachings of the New Testament and turned Christian liberty into unbridled license. Christian liberty is not the right to live as we please. It is freedom from self and Satan in order that we can bring glory to God in our lives.

The Lord concluded this letter with a statement that appears in all the correspondence to these churches: **Let anyone who has ears to hear listen to what the Spirit says to the churches**. The repetition of this admonishment in each letter reminds us of the necessity to keep our hearts open to the leading of the Holy Spirit.

This admonition describes the three kinds of believers who would read or hear this prophecy. It is not speaking of literal "ears," but of the hearts of those who would read or hear. It describes (1) those who are not responsive to the Holy Spirit and are not saved; (2) those who are believers but are unable to hear from the Spirit because of compromise in their lives. Many believers are unwilling to hear from the Spirit of God; (3) those spiritually minded believers who joyfully hear and respond to what the Spirit of God says.

The Divine Promise to the Church (Rev. 2:7b)

The letter to the Ephesian church ends with a promise to those who are faithful and victorious, as each of the letters to the other churches end. This promise is simple: **To the one who conquers, I will give the right to eat from the tree of life, which is in the paradise of God.** Paige Patterson remarks in his volume on Revelation, "Each of the promises for overcoming [needs to be understood] in the light of [Revelation] 12:11, 'They overcame him / by the blood of the Lamb / and by the word of their testimony.'" [2] There are two reasons for the believer's victory: the blood of the Lamb and the word of their testimony. These are the keys to victory!

Strengths and Weaknesses

Review Revelation 2:1-7. List the strengths and weaknesses of the church in Ephesus.

Strengths:

Weaknesses:

Christ's condemnation of the church in Ephesus was that they had "abandoned the love" they had at first. What habits or actions in our lives might contribute toward us abandoning our love for Christ and our love for others?

Interestingly, the Artemision contained a special tree in the center of that temple. It was sometimes referred to as the tree of life. Citizens of Ephesus would be familiar with that tree which was attractive for its promised long life. Now the Lord spoke of another tree of life. When God created the garden of Eden, He placed the tree of life in the "middle of the garden, as well as the tree of the knowledge of good and evil" (Gen. 2:8-9). Adam and Eve were forbidden to eat of that tree. When their disobedience occurred, God made it impossible to eat of that tree again: "He drove the man out and stationed the cherubim and the flaming, whirling sword east of the garden of Eden to guard the way to the tree of life" (3:24).

Now the Lord declared that victorious believers have **the right to eat from the tree of life, which is in the paradise of God.** The tree created by God and placed in the paradise that was the garden of Eden has been transplanted to the "paradise of God." Patterson says "[Paradise] occurs only three times in the New Testament.... [In] the three occasions ... 'paradise' is synonymous with the unique dwelling place of God or heaven."[3]

When Jesus told the thief on the cross, "Truly I tell you, today you will be with me in paradise" (Luke 23:43), He was describing the dwelling place of God. These overcoming saints in Ephesus were given the same assurance by our Lord as He concluded this letter to the church of Ephesus.

A CLOSER LOOK

Ephesus

Situated beautifully at the mouth of the Cayster River and the harbor to the Aegean Sea, Ephesus rose gently up the inclines of two prominent mountains. The city itself was easy to defend and was the open door to the profitable trade routes in the east. It was the most vital commercial center of Asia Minor.

When Rome conquered the city in 189 BC, it gave the city to the king of Pergamum as a reward to his military support. The last king of Pergamum died in 133 BC and the city then came completely under Roman control.

As the capital city of the Roman Province of Asia, Ephesus was the home of the Roman governor. It was also a strong proponent of emperor worship which abounded throughout the Roman Empire.

The earliest inhabitants from the area of Ephesus were driven out about 1000 BC by Ionian settlers led by Androclus of Athens. As the Greeks settled, they established the native religion that involved the worship of Artemis, the goddess of fertility. Known as Artemis by the Greeks and Diana by the Romans, her worship was the most dominant worship in all of Asia Minor.

Personal Reflection

1. Jesus issued some very complimentary commendations to the church at Ephesus in Revelation 2:2-3. As you reflect on your life, which of these might He compliment you on? Which would He not likely have complimentary words to speak about you? Explain.

2. Jesus also condemned the church for having abandoned its first love. How can we tell if someone has abandoned his or her first love of Jesus? What do you learn about yourself when you apply those measures to your life?

3. What significance do you see in the promise Jesus made in verse 7 to those who conquer?

1. John Phillips, *Exploring Revelation* (Chicago: Moody Press, 1974) 51.
2. Paige Patterson, *Revelation,* The New American Commentary, Volume 39 (Nashville: B&H, 2012) 89.
3. Ibid., 90-91.

SMYRNA

REVELATION 2:8-11

Smyrna was a free city which allowed it to have its own governmental control. It was the first city in the world to build a temple to honor Rome. In AD 26 when the cities of Asia Minor were competing for the privilege of erecting a temple for the worship of the EmperorTiberius, Smyrna was chosen to build it, her reward for loyalty over more than a century. Smyrna was famous in the ancient world for its beauty and its loyalty to Rome.

It must have been startling to those in Smyrna when the Lord Jesus Christ began His letter be referring to Himself as **the First and the Last**. In comparison to the magnificence of the Lord, earthly splendor and value becomes both useless and worthless. Competing for earthly recognition was nothing when compared to the eternal reality found in Jesus Christ.

The church at Smyrna existed in the midst of terrifying pressure. The name *Smyrna* comes from a root meaning "bitter," symbolic of the enormous persecution the church faced. It is identified with myrrh which was used for embalming the dead. Myrrh was fragrant when it was crushed, a further description of the crushing attacks the church faced.

Smyrna was a difficult and perplexing place to maintain a Christian testimony. "Domitian was on the throne. He was a suspicious and blasphemous tyrant. The time had come for the second round of official persecution to begin. In his second letter, John addresses a church which was soon to face the bitter hatred of the world.The church at Smyrna became the cameo of the church under fire."[1]

That persecution reached its ultimate expression in the martyrdom of Polycarp, the bishop of Smyrna. He was the last person known to have talked with John, and he was burned at the stake in AD 155 after decades of persecution.

What's in a Name?

Identify from the following passages various names by which Jesus is known:

Isaiah 9:6 –

Isaiah 9:6 –

Isaiah 9:6 –

Isaiah 9:6 –

Isaiah 59:20 –

Matthew 1:23 –

John 1:29 –

John 6:35 –

John 8:12 –

John 10:9 –

John 10:11 –

John 11:25 –

John 14:6 –

1 Corinthians 10:4 —

1 Timothy 1:1 —

How do these various names help you better understand who Jesus is?

Greatly Needed Comfort (Rev. 2:8-9)

The introduction of Jesus in this passage is one that speaks of supernatural power. The title **First and the Last** expresses the splendor of His character. All seven of these letters magnify the Lord Jesus. The descriptions of Christ express the highest view of Christology in the Scripture. He is, indeed, the Lord Jesus Christ!

That title the First and the Last was used as a title for God in the Old Testament (see Isa. 44:6; 48:12). It would speak volumes to the hearts of the Smyrnian believers. Christ was clearly identifying Himself as divine.

He is **the one who was dead and came to life**, which literally means "one who was a corpse, yet lives." He possesses power over death itself! He knew what the Smyrna believers were experiencing because He lived through the same kind of suffering. He is the First and the Last and in spite of death, He still lives! "This church is in the midst of a great sorrow, and the Lord announces Himself as the living One Who has passed through death, and therefore possesses the keys of death and of Hades."[2]

The believers lived in dangerous and desperate times. The pressure to embrace the worship of the emperor and the libelous, slanderous accusations of the Jews made life devastating for them. But the very title Jesus used would be celebrated. The church was despised, considered traitors to Rome, and violently persecuted. They did not worship in magnificent temples, but in caves, catacombs, and hidden places. No matter how things developed in Smyrna, the risen Christ was with them!

This is the same message the apostle Paul proclaimed in Romans 8. After listing all the things that could threaten believers, He declared that there was nothing in this world or anywhere in the universe that could separate believers from the love of God in Jesus Christ (Rom. 8:35-39).

Here is a letter to all people, in all times, who have faced disappointment and persecution and have known the devastation of depression and despair.

Not a word of condemnation for this church! The only other church not to face words of censure was the church in Philadelphia. Most of the letters contain commendations for the church and then a denunciation. But to the church in Smyrna there is no word of disapproval.

The comfort that Jesus gave this persecuted church was superb and extraordinary. **I know your affliction and poverty, but you are rich. I know the slander of those who say they are Jews and are not, but are a synagogue of Satan.**

Jesus began with the most comforting two words anyone could ever hear: "I know." There were two basic words in the Greek language which are translated "to know." One means "to begin to know." The word Jesus used here is the other and means "to know in a full and complete manner." He knew what they were going through in a most complete and thorough way because He experienced it Himself in the events of His journey to the cross. He was also going through it with them.

This is a powerful word of comfort from our Lord Jesus Christ for every believer. Whatever we face, whether it is threats, oppression, opposition, persecution, torment, or attacks,

Below: Roman arch in the agora at ancient Smyrna dates from the 1st centuries BC and AD.

ILLUSTRATOR PHOTO/ BOB SCHATZ (11/26/4)

Jesus knows because He is there with us. "For we do not have a high priest who is unable to sympathize with our weaknesses, but one who has been tempted in every way as we are, yet without sin" (Heb. 4:15). He has promised to be with us throughout our earthly journey (13:5).

Nothing hurts me that does not hurt Him. When I am attacked, He is attacked. Jesus is with me in every moment of my life. What a word of comfort and encouragement for these embattled saints and for us!

Affliction denotes pressure, a strong word for brutal attacks and oppression. In classical Greek, "it is, for instance, used of a man who was tortured to death by being slowly crushed by a great boulder laid on him."[3] It is the word that could be used of the stone that grinds the wheat until it is crushed or the pressing of grapes until the juice flows freely. It speaks of unspeakable pressure upon an individual.

Then He said, **I know your ... poverty.** That word actually means "destitution." They were not just poor in the sense they had enough to eat but had nothing extra. They did not have anything. They were the poorest of the poor. They had nothing of this world's goods. Smyrna was one of the wealthiest cities in the world, yet these Smyrnian believers were destitute.

Even though great wealth abounded, poverty was prevalent in the church. Many of the believers were from the lower class or slaves in Smyrna. The gulf between the wealthy and the poor was more extreme than it is in the world today. In many instances their homes had been destroyed and they were left homeless and helpless in a dangerous city. But they still had God! They were **rich** in Him.

Someone has observed that the early churches were marked by material poverty and spiritual strength. Churches today seem to be noted for their material wealth and spiritual weakness.

But you are rich. The word for "rich" is the root of our word *plutocrat*. Vance Havner said, "These Smyrna saints were the Lord's plutocrats."[4] What a reminder of the incomparable riches we have in Christ. No circumstances can destroy those riches. "For you know the grace of our Lord Jesus Christ: Though he was rich, for your sake he became poor, so that by his poverty you might become rich" (2 Cor. 8:9). Every injustice and hostility they faced here on earth would produce an even greater reward in heaven (4:17).

Then He said, **I know the slander** you face. The word for "slander" is the Greek word from which we get our English word *blasphemy*. Normally that word refers to slander against God. But here it describes the blasphemous, slanderous, and libelous statements being made about the believers in the church.

There were six basic accusations hurled at the Christians: (1) they refused to worship Caesar, so were accused of disloyalty to Rome; (2) they spoke of eating the body and drinking the blood of Christ, so were thought to be cannibals; (3) their "love feasts" gave rise to the claim that they were extremely immoral; (4) they did not believe in the Greek gods, so were labeled atheists; (5) they spoke of the fire of the spirit and the fires of divine judgment, so were accused of arson; (6) their loyalty to Jesus Christ was stronger than traditional family ties, resulting in many Jews disowning family members who embraced Christianity. The charge of dividing families was hurled at them.

Along with ever-present and growing hostility from Roman authorities was the aggressive resentment of the large Jewish community, which was the originator of many of the accusations. This immense belligerence toward Christians was because many in the Jewish community were being converted to faith in Jesus Christ. This created great animosity among the unconverted Jews.

The Lord Jesus described these slanderous Jews as **a synagogue of Satan.** They had viciously slandered the believers in Smyrna in a way that was a clear violation of Jewish law itself. They attacked Christians for the sake of their own prosperity and comfort. The Lord Jesus quickly accused them of merely claiming to be Jews, while not actually living by their own standards.

These Jews did everything they could to push for aggressive persecution of Christians by Rome. It was not the first time this had happened. It was the Jews who initiated opposition to the Christians in Antioch (Acts 13:50), in Iconium (14:2), in Lystra (v. 19), and in Thessalonica (17:5). About AD 90 the Jews circulated a libelous document to get rid of the growing threat of Christian converts.

Along with this document, the Emperor Domitian greatly increased his efforts to make Emperor worship mandatory and get rid of all objectors. Christians were left in a dilemma. They had existed as a sub-culture of Judaism but had never had approved status on their own. Now they faced incredible pressure to deny Christ and adopt Judaism in order to avoid serious suffering from both Rome and the Jews.

No examination of ancient Smyrna is complete without knowing of the climax of this persecution in AD 155 with the martyrdom of Polycarp, the bishop of Smyrna. He had a dream in which he saw the pillow under his head burning with fire. Upon waking he told his followers, "I must be burnt alive."

Betrayed by a young slave who broke down under torture, Polycarp was arrested and brought before the proconsul in the city. He was given the choice of cursing the name of Christ or offering a sacrifice of worship to Caesar.

To refuse to pay homage to Caesar would result in death. His firm resolve was dramatically found in his reply: "Eighty and six years have I served Him and He has done me no wrong. How can I blaspheme my King who saved me?"

When threatened with burning at the stake, Polycarp replied, "You threaten me with the fire that burns for a time, and is quickly quenched, for you do not know the fire which awaits the wicked in the judgment to come and in everlasting punishment. Why are you waiting? Come, do what you will." Polycarp died more than 50 years after the severe persecution of believers began in Smyrna, the climax of one of the most vicious persecutions in history.

Jesus said, **I know,** regarding all the brutal opposition to the church at Smyrna. What a needed comfort to understand that our Lord Jesus Christ knows! We can praise God that our Savior knows our pain, hurt, disappointments, and suffering.

Promise of Continued Suffering (Rev. 2:10a)

One would think that after acknowledging all the affliction believers at Smyrna were going through, Jesus would say, "Cheer up, it is going to get better." But instead, He said, "Cheer up, it's going to get worse!" There will be continued persecution and brutal attacks. It isn't going to get better right now. Tough days are ahead. It's going to be a rough ride.

We often adopt the idea that to be blessed by God is to receive material values and good health. Surely our God will not let us have sickness, accidents, rejection, hostility, or opposition. We want to believe that if we receive the Lord into our hearts everything will be wonderful. The only problem with that is that it just is not true. That is our conclusion, not God's. Jesus declared just the opposite, but told the believers **Don't be afraid of what you are about to suffer.**

He was saying, "The past was bad enough, but the road ahead will be worse. The suffering will only get more intense and painful. What you have experienced is preliminary to what lies ahead."

They would face imprisonment, **affliction,** and some would even experience death. Jesus was speaking of the whole gamut of difficulties they would face. It would be harassment, accusations, slander, exile, trials, fines, and execution.

Why would these things happen? Jesus simply said, it was **to test you.** Faith needs to be tested to reveal its strength. Faith is not tested when we are healthy, when all is going well, or when there are no challenges or difficulties for us to face. The testing of our Christian character comes when the roof collapses, when life falls in around us, and suffering comes. What then?

The time is coming for each of us when we must be tested. We need to hear Jesus say, **Don't be afraid of what you are about to suffer.** Jesus said that **you will experience affliction for ten days.** Some try to apply this statement to some long-term persecution that occurred in history. I believe it simply means that God is going to limit what will happen to them. It will be heavy and hard, but there will be an end. It is dark tonight but morning is coming!

Since it pleased God to make the Captain of our salvation perfect through suffering (see Heb. 2:10), we should expect to walk through the valley of testing ourselves.

Reward for Faithful Believers (Rev. 2:10b-11)

The Lord promised, **Be faithful to the point of death, and I will give you the crown of life.** Testing and suffering does not have the last word. Jesus comforts us through it all, but He promises that we will conquer at last. Our future is secure, not in what we do, but in what God has done, and what He has provided for us for the eternity ahead.

"The famous golden street that wound up to Mount Pagus ... was studded like a crown with various ... architectural achievement. Therefore, for Smyrnians to speak of the city itself as 'the crown' was not unusual. But the Lord's message to [believers] is that the city may be a crown [of beauty]; but a permanent crown of life, crown enduring forever, would be the gift of the risen Christ to those who were faithful even to death."[5]

The nature of the crown faithful believers will receive is vitally important. It is not the crown worn by royalty. That crown was called a diadem. This crown is the *stephanos*, which is the victor's crown. It was the laurel wreath given to the athlete who won an event in competition. It was, also, the celebration crown worn at marriages. It speaks of victory and joy which comes to faithful believers.

The writer of Hebrews declared, "Therefore, since we also have such a large cloud of witnesses surrounding us, let us lay aside every hinderance and the sin that so easily ensnares us. Let us run with endurance the race that lies before us" (Heb. 12:1). God has placed us in a race. Jesus declared that those who are faithful through the journey set before them will receive the victor's crown.

The Lord cautioned the Smyrna church again to **let anyone who has ears to hear listen to what the Spirit says to the churches.** Genuine believers must always be sensitive to the voice of the Holy Spirit. Faithful believers will be victorious over every obstacle. They will be rewarded with the victor's crown and with eternal security as they **will never be harmed by the second death.**

Some of them could expect to be martyred. Physical death is not to be feared, because "we are confident, and we would prefer to be away from the body and at home with the Lord" (2 Cor. 5:8). Regardless of what happens in the first death, faithful believers will never be affected by the second death.

The second death is reserved for those who will stand before the Lord at the great white throne judgment. They will be condemned because they have refused to receive the offer of salvation. They are there because their names are not found in the Lamb's book of life. Their destiny is to be cast into the lake of fire, the second death.

Unless the Lord returns first, we will all die once physically. If we are born again, we will never die twice. Those who receive the free gift of eternal life offered by the Lord Jesus will never experience this second death, which means an eternity of separation from God in hell. There is no relief from the agony of being lost from God's presence. They will be always dying, but never dead. All the pain we can imagine in the second death will never be relieved by dying. It is an eternal death designed for those who reject Jesus Christ.

In His remarkable prayer on the evening before His crucifixion, Jesus prayed for "those who believe in me through their [the disciples'] word" (John 17:20). He continued to pray for all of us who would be saved through that message: "Father, I want those you have given me to be with me where I am, so that they will see my glory, which you have given me because you loved me before the world's foundation" (v. 24).

No danger from the second death awaits believers. We will be in His presence, enraptured by His glory throughout eternity!

A CLOSER LOOK

Smyrna

Situated impressively at the end of the road crossing from Lydia and Phrygia, Smyrna dominated commercial business from the rich valley of the Hermus River. It was recognizably the second most important city in Asia Minor, close to Ephesus in its significance. The city had a small land-locked harbor which rested in the center of the city. It was a well-protected harbor which made it safe and convenient to the entire city.

Smyrna was known as the most beautiful city in all of Asia. It was called the fairest of cities, the ornament of Asia, the flower of Asia, and the crown of Asia.[6]

In 600 BC it was conquered by the Lydians and for 400 years was no city at all, but just a group of small villages. About 200 BC Lysimachus rebuilt it as a

Inseparable

John's words to the believers in Smyrna echo similar words from Paul in Romans 8:35-39:

> *35 Who can separate us from the love of Christ? Can affliction or distress or persecution or famine or nakedness or danger or sword? 36 As it is written:*
>
> > *Because of you*
> > *we are being put to death all day long;*
> > *we are counted as sheep to be slaughtered.*
>
> *37 No, in all these things we are more than conquerors through him who loved us. 38 For I am persuaded that neither death nor life, nor angels nor rulers, nor things present nor things to come, nor powers, 39 nor height nor depth, nor any other created thing will be able to separate us from the love of God that is in Christ Jesus our Lord.*

The message of Revelation 2:8-11 and Romans 8:35-39 are the same: N O T H I N G can separate us from God's love. Maybe you've experienced something like ...

- *an unexpected health problem*
- *a broken family relationship*
- *a disappointment in your job*
- *a funeral for someone you loved*
- *a child whose choices disappoint you*

How does knowing that you can never be separated from God's love encourage your faith today?

planned city, which was unique in the ancient world. Very few cities were built with such specifications. The remarkable streets were wide and straight and adorned with magnificent buildings. Mount Pagus looked like a crown atop the main street and made a spectacular and breathtaking picture to those who came into the harbor, as it was the first thing seen.

Personal Reflection

1. What significance does the fact Jesus is "the First and the Last" have on your life?

2. In what ways do you experience "affliction and poverty"? Would Jesus say of you, "But you are rich"? Explain.

3. Twice in verse 9 Jesus told the believers in Smyrna "I know," regarding their affliction and poverty and the slander they faced. What does it mean to you that Jesus knows what you are facing?

1. John Phillips, *Exploring Revelation* (Chicago: Moody Press, 1974) 54.
2. G. Campbell Morgan, *A First Century Message to Twentieth Century Christians* (New York: Fleming H. Revell, 1902) 58.
3. William Barclay, *Letters to the Seven Churches* (Nashville: Abingdon Press, 1947) 35.
4. Vance Havner, *Repent of Else* (New York: Fleming H. Revell, 1958) 33.
5. Paige Patterson, *Revelation,* The New American Commentary, Volume 39 (Nashville: B&H, 2012) 98.
6. William Barclay, *The Revelation of John*, Revised Edition (Philadelphia: Westminster Press, 1976) 73.

PERGAMUM

REVELATION 2:12-17

The city of Pergamum was known as the Citadel, which referred to its location on a high hill overlooking the valley. It was a very distinctive city but it was not a great commercial city. There were no vast trade routes, no huge harbors. It was not a city known for its commerce, trade, or politics. Its importance in part was that parchment was invented and produced in Pergamum and was widely used in those days.

The Lord was rightly concerned about preserving and spreading the truth. This letter warned about heretical teaching and immorality which flowed from all the strange ideas about religion espoused there. There was also a large temple, known as the Red Basilica, to the god Isis or Serapis. It is likely that the church at Pergamum met in the main building of the Red Basilica.

Jesus introduced Himself in this letter as **the one who has the sharp, double-edged sword**. The highest symbol of authority in ancient days was the sword. It represented the greatest power the people knew. It referred to absolute supremacy. To this city that had so many religious symbols of dominance, Jesus declared that He had all authority.

Faithful in Satan's Stronghold (Rev. 2:13)

The Lord was keenly aware that the believers in Pergamum were surrounded by paganism and were exposed to all kinds of coercion from the evil culture there. He began with, **I know where you live—where Satan's throne is.** Satan not only dwelt in Pergamum, but he ruled it! It was his evil domain. One would have had difficulty finding any place where the anti-God forces were more authoritative or powerful. Even amid Satan's throne, this church was a faithful, working, and dedicated church. Because of Satan the world is forever the enemy of God.

The Lord spoke of the "synagogue of Satan" that was present in Smyrna (v. 9) and Philadelphia (3:9). But about Pergamum we read that Satan's throne was there. Where Satan's throne is established, "the peril that threatens the church is not so much that of direct opposition as that of patronage ... entering into alliance with the forces under [Satan's] control."[1]

Wherever there is a materialistic, sensual, and lustful city, Satan is always there in power. The church has the only message that can defeat Satan. Heresy can only be destroyed by truth. This church remained true to the Lord even in the presence of Satan's power, and Jesus commended them for that.

It is vitally important for us to remember that our Lord knows where we live. He knows our name, our address, our zip code, and every other bit of information about us. It is also important for us to remember that physical persecution is not the only form of opposition we will face. Immorality, compromise, false teachers, and false teaching stalk our churches every day!

The church at Pergamum found itself in a position where it could easily have drifted into worldliness and compromise. Caution! We never drift anywhere worth going! Our movement must always be driven on the wings of devotion and not on the whims of the currents around us.

Nevertheless, they were **holding on to my name.** They were loyal to the name of the Lord Jesus Christ. His name is synonymous with Himself. The

name of God and of Christ always represents His nature and character.

His name represents the truth about who He is and what He has done. It is a strong reminder of His full humanity and full deity. It also was expressive of His redemptive work brought through His death on Calvary. The church at Pergamum confirmed Jesus Christ as Lord. They honored His character and redeeming power.

Further, **you ... did not deny your faith in me.** They had not betrayed the purpose for which the Lord Jesus Christ came. They testified to His redemptive purpose and had complete confidence in His mission and atoning work. They had not turned their backs on the gospel. This underscores the fact that He is both Savior and Lord! We must not only cling to His name but also exercise faith in Him.

There had already been at least one believer killed because of his devotion to Christ. His name was **Antipas** and he paid for his courageous stand for Christ with his very life. The primary religious threat in Pergamum was the imperial worship of Rome and its Caesars. Because Antipas would not take an oath and burn incense to Rome, he lost his life. This is the end result of the activity of Satan's authority.

Jesus called Antipas **my faithful witness.** Of special note is that this same title is given to Jesus Himself in Revelation 1:5. No higher word could have been spoken of this martyr in Pergamum!

Like Antipas, we are called to stand whatever the situation, and stand we must as God's people. Regardless of the appeal of the seduction, of the undertow of the tide, of the brutality of the attacks, or of the fearfulness of the threats, as God's people we must stand, faithful only and always to Jesus, our Lord and our God.

Remember that the city of Pergamum was famous for its medical hospital and school, and for the temple of Asclepios. The symbol of Asclepios was the intertwining of serpents that even today is the symbol of the medical profession. The worship of Asclepios took a very sinister turn with its slogan, "Asclepios Soter," meaning Asclepios is Savior. Pergamum coins had the emblem of the intertwined serpents on them. This was another attack on the salvation the young church proclaimed in Satan's domain.

Left: The theater at Pergamum dating from the 2nd century BC. The theater has 80 rows with a seating capacity of 10,000.

ILLUSTRATOR PHOTO/ BOB SCHATZ (11/27/14)

"Christians at Pergamum proved that it was perfectly possible to be a Christian under such circumstances. Even when martyrdom was in the air they did not flinch."[2]

Misunderstanding Christian Liberty (Rev. 2:14-15)

Now the entire mood of this letter changes. The praise and commendations ceased. From every outward appearance, the believers at Pergamum were a thriving and healthy congregation. Now the rebuke and the warning came on strong. Their tolerance of heresy is now clearly condemned.

They were "holding" on to Christ's name (v. 13), but there were some **who hold to the teaching of Balaam ... [and] of the Nicolaitans.** The same Greek verb for *hold* is used in all three instances. While most held onto the name of Christ, there were some in the church who just as tenaciously held on to heresy. Despite their overall faithfulness and loyalty to the name of the Lord Jesus Christ, there was compromise with false doctrine. That problem existed then and it is even more pervasive today.

The doctrines of Balaam and of the Nicolaitans carried similar false teachings. The first mention of the Nicolaitans was to the church at Ephesus (v. 6). There the church was commended because it hated "the practices of the Nicolaitans," which the Lord also hates. But here the reference is to the **teaching of the Nicolaitans.** "The deeds of the Nicolaitans are mentioned in the letter to Ephesus. The deeds had by now become a doctrine. What was at first tolerated as an unscriptural practice is now accepted as an unscriptural principle."[3]

These twin heresies were leading the church to compromise the truth of the gospel and the full devotion required of every believer. While there is uncertainty about the exact content of these heresies, many Christian scholars have suggested that these two false doctrines were taught by the same teachers. Both resulted in spiritual compromise. What Balaam had done against the Israelites of the Old Testament, the Nicolaitans evidently had done in Pergamum and other locales in the New Testament. They considered the liberty with which Christ has freed His followers as a liberty to sin.

Compromise usually means an easing of friction between two parties. Compromise is used to settle differences and not to stir things up. This church was faithful and believed the right things about Jesus Christ, even under the opposition of Satan's dominance. It was a strong church and an orthodox church. They had not denied the Lord, but they were tolerating heresy.

In the name of benevolence, they had tolerated what should have been expelled. They had maintained fellowship with those who did deny the Lord. That was the problem that Jesus addressed to this church. They had allowed the teachings of Balaam and the Nicolaitans to remain in the church. Those doctrines taught by Balaam and the Nicolaitans were as simple as attacking the

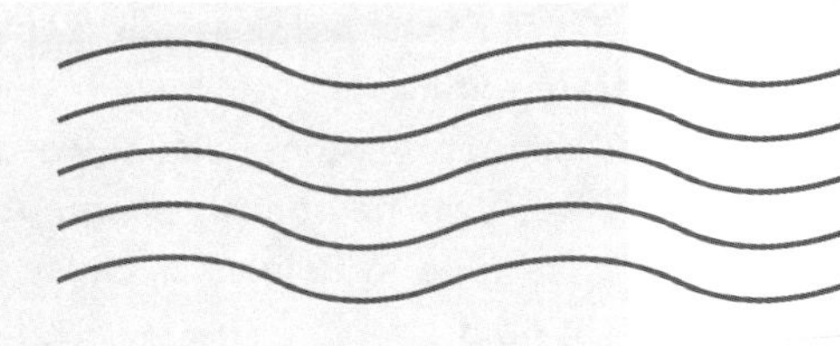

Spiritual Compromise

"Despite their overall faithfulness and loyalty to the name of the Lord Jesus Christ, there was compromise with false doctrine. That problem existed then and it is even more pervasive today."

The church at Pergamum held fast to the teachings of Christ while at the same time holding fast to the messages of false teachers.

When is compromise a good thing?

When is compromise a bad thing?

List examples of ways the culture today tempts us to compromise the truth of the gospel:

standards of holiness and separation from evil that God demands His people to maintain.

Remember that Balaam was called by a king to curse Israel (see Num. 22–24). Every time he opened his mouth to curse Israel, he blessed Israel. It became so frustrating to Balaam because he was offered money to curse Israel but could not do it.

Apparently, Balaam thought that though he could not curse Israel, he could counsel Israel to compromise the purposes of God by intermarrying with the Moabites. He did not curse the nation, he just encouraged them to compromise the purposes of God. By doing so he caused the people to tolerate immorality and heresy, and many engaged in both (see Num. 25; 31:13-16).

The end result was that this false teaching became a national disgrace in Israel. The result in Pergamum was the idea that one could believe the right things about Jesus Christ and then do anything one wanted to do. The church had quietly slipped into the idea that orthodox belief was all that was important and conduct did not matter. There were at least three things being taught in Pergamum: pagan idolatry, sexual immorality, and spiritual compromise. They were being taught that purity of life and conduct was not required by God of all believers. That was the doctrine of Balaam and the Nicolaitans.

The Book of Numbers suggests that there were compromising and immoral individuals who followed Balaam's advice (vv. 15-16). In every age, God's people have faced the challenge of dealing with heresy and immorality. That is a reality in every age and in every church. The battle for truth is never ended till Jesus comes again!

That's why Jude, in his dynamic epistle, said, "I found it necessary to write, appealing to you to contend for the faith that was delivered to the saints once for all" (Jude 3). Every generation must be alert for heresy and false teaching and carefully deal with them from the Word of God. Though Satan was defeated at the cross, he and his minions continue to resist every advance into their evil dominion. John Stott concludes, "The kingdom of Satan retreats only as the kingdom of God advances."[4]

Jesus identified Himself as "the one who has the sharp, double-edged sword" (Rev. 2:12). That double-edged sword extended from His mouth (1:16) and is a symbol of the truth He has spoken. It is His Word, thus, it is the Word of God. It may have been a reminder that the Old Testament Balaam was killed with a sword (see Num. 31:8). Those who followed Balaam in Pergamum would suffer a similar fate if they did not repent. The only difference would be that now the sword would be the Word of Christ.

A Command with a Warning (Rev. 2:16)

So repent! Otherwise, I will come to you quickly and fight against them with the sword of my mouth. That sword is the Word of God. It is the effective work of that sword that convicts of sin, confronts individuals with the truth, and offers a chance to respond to truth. It is also that which brings assurance of the salvation received.

The Lord demanded repentance. It is amazing that He was not talking to the false teachers of Balaam and the Nicolaitans. He was calling the church to repent. They were not guilty of believing those things, but were guilty of tolerating those who were guilty.

It was imperative to remove those who embraced this heresy from the church. Christ essentially said, "You either take care of it or I'll come and do it Myself." His warning was striking: **I will come to you quickly and fight against them with the sword of my mouth.** He called the church to either judge these heretics or He would come and judge them. Christ's greatest wrath is against those who lead others astray and teach them to sin.

The Lord was calling the church to exclude those people from fellowship. His statement was not that He would fight against the believers in Pergamum, but that He would fight against those who perpetrated the heresy. Justice and mercy are both seen in this call to repentance. The church must not give the false teachers false security. The heresy being taught was wrong and would destroy the church.

Look closely at Paul's decisive word in Romans 1:28,32: "Because they did not think it worthwhile to acknowledge God, God delivered them over to a corrupt mind so that they do what is not right ... Although they know God's just sentence—that those who practice such things deserve to die—they not only do them, but even applaud others who practice them." Committing sin is grievous, but to teach it and applaud the sins of others is strictly forbidden. That is the great tragedy of compromise. Soon half-truths become whole heresy!

Hidden Manna and a New Name (Rev. 2:17)

Two significant gifts are promised **to the one who conquers**: **Hidden manna** and **a white stone** will be the reward to the overcomer. The first describes the spiritual food provided by God in His Word. This indicated individual feeding, not a church function. Manna divinely appeared each day, yet human gathering was required. God gave it, but the people had to go get it.

This is the beauty of the role of the Word of God in the lives of believers. All truth is gathered in the Word, but for many it is "hidden" because they have not gathered it for themselves. If they will gather it, the Holy Spirit will apply it to their lives. This certainly looks to the heavenly feast that believers will enjoy in heaven with the Lord Himself.

Then the Lord Jesus Christ said, **I will also give him a white stone, and on the stone a new name is inscribed that no one knows except the one who receives it. White stone** represents the believers' purity of life and the holiness of God. The new name doubtless represents the name that believers receive in Jesus Christ. We do not know the identity of that name, but it will be a "new name."

The Greek language has two words for *new*. One refers to new in time, while the other, used here, speaks of new in kind or nature. The word here speaks of something that has never been seen before. That word is also dominant in the Book of Revelation: we have a "new name" (2:17; see 3:12); new Jerusalem (3:12; 21:2); new song (5:9; 14:3); new heavens and new earth (21:1); and God makes all things new (21:5). All of these new things are new in kind. Revelation is describing a completely new world!

In ancient times there were some beautiful uses of white stone. Sometimes it was given to a man after a trial when he was acquitted. The stone showed that he was not guilty. After a battle, the victor on returning home from the battlefield would be given a white stone representing victory. It was also used to give to a person granted citizenship which signified his new status. Good friends would often take a white stone and break it. Each would write his name on that stone, which signified their friendship, and it would be passed down through the generations.

For believers, the Lord Jesus Christ said that we are judged righteous and acquitted before God through Jesus Christ. The white stone signifies the triumph of the child of God over all enemies. The white stone of citizenship indicates our free entrance into the city of God. The white stone of unending friendship indicates our relationship with the Lord Himself. When we faithfully obey Him we get a white stone with a new name and hidden manna that only God can give.

The Lord promised that He would write **a new name** on that stone. "Whatever the stone may be, the new name to be engraved on it is undoubtedly the name of Christ, who says later in his letter to the Philadelphian church: 'I will also write on him my new name' (Rev. 3:12)."[5]

The color white is a word that speaks of dazzling brightness and purity. It is the dominant color in Revelation. It is seen as: "white as wool—white as snow" (1:14); "white stone" (2:17); "white clothes" (3:5; 4:4); "white robe(s)" (6:11; 7:9); "white horse(s)" (6:2; 19:14); "white cloud" (14:14); "white linen" (19:14); and "white throne" (20:11).

The Sword

"So repent! Otherwise, I will come to you quickly and fight against them with the sword of my mouth" (Rev. 2:16).

Match each reference to the description it gives of the power of God's Word.

Isaiah 40:8	*"a light on my path"*
Jeremiah 15:16	*"power of God for salvation"*
Psalm 18:30	*"sharper than any double-edged sword"*
Psalm 19:7-8	*"a delight to me"*
Psalm 119:105	*"inspired by God"*
Matthew 24:35	*"pure"*
Romans 1:16	*"perfect" "trustworthy" "right" "radiant"*
2 Timothy 3:16	*"remains forever"*
Hebrews 4:12	*"will never pass away"*

It must, however, be clearly understood that the church of Jesus Christ must not tolerate within her borders those who would compromise God's standards of truth, turning the white to black.

A CLOSER LOOK

Pergamum

Pergamum was primarily a religious city. "Here a pitched battle was being fought, in which the combatants were not people but ideas. The issue was not between good and evil, but between truth and error."[6] In those days it was believed that every weird idea that was forced out of any place would end up in Pergamum. The city thrived on religious ideas and concepts. There was a multiplicity of pagan doctrines expounded and the city was consumed with desire for wealth and fashion.

It was about 16 miles from the coast and had a Greek theater that would seat 10,000 built into the very steep slope of the terrain rising out of the city. It had the second best library in ancient Greece with over 200,000 volumes. The Upper Acropolis stood 1000 feet above the plain of the River Caicus. It held the large theater and library, in addition to the marketplace, palace and barracks for the soldiers. All of this rested comfortably near the altar of Zeus. That is likely the area that John referred to as "Satan's throne" in Revelation 2:13.

Personal Reflection

1. Jesus identified Himself to the church at Pergamum as "the one who has the sharp, double-edged sword." That description reflects the fact He has all authority. Evaluate your life over the past few months. To what degree have you lived as if Jesus has all authority?

2. The writer makes the observation that "we never drift anywhere worth going! Our movement must always be driven on the wings of devotion and not on the whims of the currents around us." How do you guard against drifting on the currents of contemporary culture?

3. The church at Pergamum was commended for holding tight to the name of Jesus and not denying their faith in Him (v. 13), but at the same time were confronted over their compromise with those who held false doctrine. In what areas of faith are you most tempted to compromise even as you hold fast in other areas of faith?

1. G. Campbell Morgan, *A First Century Message to Twentieth Century Christians* (New York: Fleming H. Revell, 1902) 87-88.
2. William Barclay, *The Revelation of John*, Revised Edition (Philadelphia: Westminster Press, 1976) 92.
3. John Phillips, *Exploring Revelation* (Chicago: Moody Press, 1974) 51.
4. John Stott, *What Christ Thinks of the Church* (London: Angus Hudson Ltd., 1990) 50.
5. Ibid., 57.
6. Ibid., 42.

THYATIRA

REVELATION 2:18-29

It is entirely possible that Lydia, the first convert from the apostle Paul's ministry in Europe, was one of the founders of this church. The city was famous for its production of a beautiful purple fabric. Lydia was selling this cloth when Paul first landed in Macedonia. Perhaps her newfound faith became her new passion to share when she returned to Thyatira. It is highly likely that she was present when this church began.

The same problems we encountered at Pergamum began to develop in Thyatira. It was the presence of a tragic toleration—allowing heresy to coexist with the truth in the church. This was a major challenge in the church. There was a woman in the church whom John called **Jezebel**. This is a reference to the extremely evil and wicked woman in Old Testament times. She was a leader in corrupting the nation of Israel morally, socially, and spiritually (see 1 Kings 18:4). Such a woman had strong influence in Thyatira.

She claimed to be a **prophetess** with absolute authority, claiming to have special insights into the deep things of God. Her perversion of the truth was being taught in the church.

It is vitally important to note how Jesus described Himself. First, He called Himself **the Son of God.** This is the first time He called Himself the Son of God in these seven letters. At the very outset He made clear that the woman was not dealing with an apostle or a prophet, but the very Son of God. He spoke as one with divine authority, and immediately established His supremacy over this woman in the church.

He also identified Himself as **the one whose eyes are like a fiery flame and whose feet are like fine bronze.** Nothing is more penetrating or consuming than fire. Everything yields before it. Everything melts in its heat.

It penetrates through and sweeps away all obstructions. Those eyes pierce the masks we often put on and search the inner recesses of our hearts, the hidden things of our souls. There is no escape from the eyes of the Lord! His assessment of the church is correct with no doubt.

His bronze feet speak of strength and judgment. This seems to be a reference to the description of Christ prophesied in Daniel 10:6. Feet move with activity and action. Christ speaks with firmness and strength of judgment in action. Sin must be judged. God cannot be silent in confronting sin. Those guilty people of Thyatira would assuredly face Him in judgment if they did not repent.

The Strength of Their Ministry (Rev. 2:19)

Thyatira was a growing, going, and advancing church. They stood by the faith. They kept on and did not get weary. They started out well and got better and better. This commendation is unprecedented. Jesus commended them for their

Below: Overview of Thyatira in modern Akhisar, Turkey. Thyatira came under Roman rule in 133 BC. Its location on the route between Pergamum and Laodicea made it an important part of the Roman road system. Thyatira, the home of Lydia, was known for its production and trade of dyes, garments, pottery, and brass objects.

ILLUSTRATOR PHOTO/ BOB SCHATZ (11/29/7)

works, love, service, faith, and patience. Unlike Ephesus, their **last works are greater than the first.**

They were a loving church. At Ephesus, they were a busy and a working church, but they had lost their first love for the Lord. Thyatira was a loving church, full of ministering works. Their effective ministry was comparable to that of the church in Ephesus, but Thyatira maintained the first love that the Ephesians abandoned.

Christ told the Ephesian church to go back and do what they used to do. Amazingly, Christ said to the Thyatiran church, **I know that your last works are greater than the first.** He told them, **I know your works—your love, faithfulness, service, and endurance.** He told them to keep on doing what they were doing and challenged them to "hold on to what you have until I come" (2:25).

The word used to identify their service is from the Greek word for *deacon.* That very word describes selfless service. There is nothing of arrogance, authority, or self-interest in that word. In fact, the word denotes one who serves for the benefit of someone else. Some serve the Lord with teeth gritted and do it because they have to do it out of a sense of duty. But not at Thyatira. Their service was loving, tender, compassionate, and unselfish. When others hurt, they hurt. They really cared about the needs of others.

Faithfulness speaks of steadfastness, dependability, and reliability. This was a church you could count on. They were going to do the right thing. Under pressure they maintained tremendous endurance and patience before God. They were not slipping backwards, nor were they even standing still. They were a church pressing steadily forward in their faith and ministry.

The church at Thyatira was similar to the one in Pergamum, as it was outwardly a thriving church with a great ministry. However, as at Pergamum, the church in Thyatira had fallen into the grip of intolerable heresy.

The Weakness of Their Fellowship (Rev. 2:20-23)

"In that fair field a poisonous weed was being allowed to luxuriate. In that healthy body a malignant cancer had begun to form. An enemy was being harboured in the midst of the fellowship."[1] Ephesus would not tolerate evil, but had lost her first love. Thyatira was strong in love, but tolerated evil. Those two extremes still exist in the church today. There is always the tendency to be strong and committed to truth while failing to love the Lord completely; or to love the Lord completely but not stand for the truth.

The Lord's complaint against this church is simple, direct, and the only issue He raised: **I have this against you: You tolerate the woman Jezebel.** The problem was that the church raised no protest against this woman. That's it. Short, direct, and devastating!

With all its good qualities, the church in Thyatira was radically deficient in holiness. "Holiness is not only God's will, but his purpose."[2] It is God's design to make all of us pure and holy believers. This thriving church allowed one woman to bring outrageous leniency and license into the church, leading many to commit immorality without rebuking or restraining her. Satan's grand strategy is to compromise our witness with scandalous conduct and blasphemous error.

Jezebel was probably not her actual name, but the mere mention of this evil woman from the Old Testament would have immediately characterized her presence for the believers. "For a woman to be called a Jezebel is every bit as bad as for a man to be called a Judas."[3] Her sinister heresy was a cancer in the body of the church. She was apparently a woman of enormous charm, persuasion, and leadership and claimed to have had special revelation from God.

The original Jezebel had lived nearly a millennium earlier. She had met a gruesome death (2 Kings 9), but her wicked spirit now appeared in the person of this devilish woman in Thyatira. Jezebel did not have a quarrel with those who wanted to worship God. Her only quarrel with Jehovah was with His monopoly. Her real evil was bringing Baal worship into Israel. In that way, she compromised and polluted the people's worship.

That was what began to happen at Thyatira. The church had a wonderful heart with a great spirit and a great vision of spreading the gospel and ministering effectively. Christ's emphasis here was on the sexual sin and compromise that was rampant in Thyatira, not upon their theology or doctrine. Little by little they began to tolerate what Jezebel taught and were led away from the purity demanded by our Covenant God.

This is such an important word for the church today. We are living in a "tolerant" society now. Intolerance is identified today as the great global sin. The Thyatiran church tolerated Jezebel, but the Lord would not tolerate their tolerance!

The presence of this subtle heresy had journeyed from Ephesus where our Lord commended believers for hating the practices of the Nicolaitans, to Pergamum where some believers followed those teachings, to Thyatira where it was tolerated by the church that lacked the discernment and courage to hold Jezebel accountable.

This was possible because much of the church did not realize what was happening (see 2:24). But the Lord knew.

That's why He described Himself as "the one whose eyes are like a fiery flame" (v. 18) and **the one who examines minds and hearts.** His flaming eyes saw all, and His response was the full fury of the One before whom all must one day stand. His unbending judgment is accurate, fair, complete, and none can endure His examination. He seems to have quoted from Jeremiah 17:10, "I, the LORD, examine the mind, I test the heart to give to each according to his way, according to what his actions deserve."

Christ told the church that He had given that evil woman **time to repent** but she refused to do so. He called upon Jezebel and her followers to repent. If she would not repent, there was still an open door for repentance with her followers. God always desires repentance of evil. But the time is coming when that door will be closed. The opportunity of a lifetime must be grasped during the lifetime of the opportunity. Our God is a patient God, but His patience will not always keep calling for repentance!

Thyatira was a great union city. Those trade unions put pressure on their members not just to organize as craftsmen, but to come together in great pagan feasts. Those feasts often included acts of idolatrous worship to pagan gods. They would usually finish the evening with a wild, licentious, sexual orgy. It was all part of their union activities. True believers could not participate in such sinfulness.

Believers in Thyatira refused to endorse any lord but Jesus. All they had to do was to bow down and say, "Caesar is Lord." In the midst of such pressure to compromise, Jezebel encouraged them to dishonor the very Lord they claimed to worship. She encouraged them to worship God, but to also worship pagan deities. "Christians cannot peacefully coexist with the world, the flesh and the devil, with Balaam and Jezebel, with worldliness and false doctrine."[4] Tolerance easily becomes compromise, then it becomes sin. There is an exclusiveness about the gospel: "There is salvation in no one else, for there is no other name under heaven given to people by which we must be saved" (Acts 4:12).

Often heresy sounds a lot like the truth. In fact, the most dangerous heresy is the one that sounds the most like the truth. Wild and weird heresy is quickly dismissed. But Satan's strategy is to deceive us with small deviations until we are led completely astray. "Any philosophy that makes it easier to sin is of the devil."[5]

The Lord was outraged at Jezebel's heresy. He said of Himself, **I am the one who examines** [present tense indicating continual examination] **minds and hearts.** He emphasized that He carefully evaluates both the thoughts and emotions of our lives. People know what we do, but Christ knows why we do it.

The Lord's judgment is seen clearly in verses 22-23, and the punishment fits the sin. To tolerate her false teaching is a sin. Jezebel and her followers face great suffering and tribulation unless they repent.

Two specific things would happen to Jezebel and her followers. Christ said, **I gave her time to repent, but she does not want to repent of her sexual immorality.** Thus, He continued, **I will throw her into a sickbed and those**

who commit adultery with her into great affliction unless they repent. "Her bed of sin will become a bed of suffering. The pleasures of sin will give place to the pains of affliction, and her spiritual offspring, too deeply dyed with her evil to be cleansed, will be killed."[6] Then Jesus warned, **Then all the churches will know that I am the one who examines minds and hearts.**

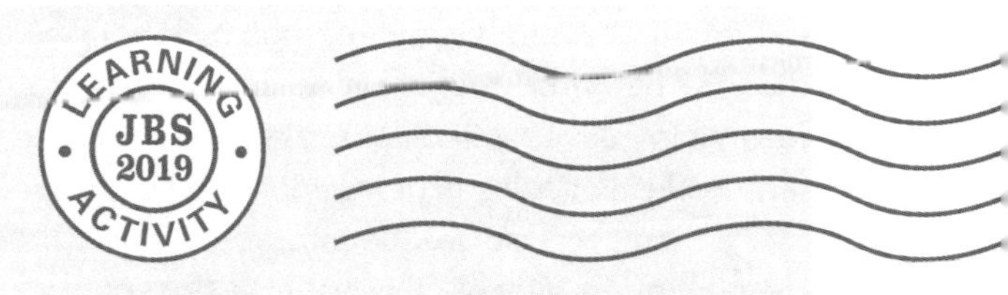

Tragic Toleration

"But I have this against you: You tolerate the woman Jezebel, who calls herself a prophetess and teaches and deceives my servants to commit sexual immorality and to eat meat sacrificed to idols" (Rev. 2:20).

"The same problems we encountered at Pergamum began to develop in Thyatira. It was the presence of a tragic toleration—allowing heresy to coexist with the truth in the church. ...
"... Tolerance easily becomes compromise, then it becomes sin."

Where do you see examples of "tragic toleration" in our communities today?

How does "tragic toleration" impact our churches?

How does it impact our families?

Christ followed this with a reminder to the faithful ones in Thyatira. He declared, **I will give to each of you according to your works.** Scripture always points to our salvation as being secured by faith in the Lord Jesus Christ. Our judgment as believers is a judgment of our works after we are saved: "For we must all appear before the judgment seat of Christ, so that each may be repaid for what he has done in the body, whether good or evil" (2 Cor. 5:10). Only the saved will appear before the judgment seat of Christ. The Great White Throne judgment is found in Revelation 20:11-15. Only unbelievers will appear at that judgment. Salvation is determined by what one has done with Jesus Christ who died for our sins. Judgment is always based upon our works. Any rewards we receive in heaven will be based upon our works. Our salvation is secured by our faith in Jesus Christ as our Savior and Lord.

The compromise Jezebel promoted was spiritual adultery and was accompanied by immorality of all varieties. Christ can never allow His church to embrace such heresy without a divine intervention!

The Message to the Faithful (Rev. 2:24-25)

God always has a faithful remnant. This was true even at Thyatira. There were devoted believers who had not embraced the heresy. To these consistent saints the Lord made a remarkable promise. **I say to the rest of you in Thyatira, who do not hold this teaching, who haven't known "the so-called secrets of Satan"—as they say—I am not putting any other burden on you. Only hold on to what you have until I come.**

Jesus mentioned the **secrets of Satan**, an obvious reference to the strategies and devices of Satan observed in Jezebel. Satan always is working to trick or deceive us and keep us away from God. That phrase could refer to the false teaching that nothing one does with one's body can destroy one's relationship with God. That opens the door to immoral, licentious, and compromising actions. It is a very subtle form of heresy.

Or the phrase could be a reference to the expansion of the doctrines of Balaam and the Nicolaitans that we have already discussed. We know that the heretical Gnostics of the first century claimed to have some deep secrets that only the elite initiates could fully understand. This title came from the Greek word for *knowledge.* These false teachers claimed to have a super knowledge that was unknown to the average person.

Christ then reminded the believers in Thyatira that they needed to cherish what they had received and not add any additional requirements on themselves. This is a strong reminder that our liberty is not freedom to do anything we choose to do, nor is it the freedom to be legalistic by requiring of others what the Scripture does not require. Don't add additional requirements to what God's Word gives us as guidelines for conduct. The Jews did this with extra-biblical laws describing how to conduct obedience to the Scriptural record.

The Lord carefully reminded the Thyratirans that no new burden was to be added to the clear instructions of His Word. Tenderly He told them to not be led astray by any new commands or liberties that some might suggest to them, regardless of the source. He reminded them that He had given them the ultimate truth, and that it was sufficient for them. Don't be led astray by those who claim superior revelation. God's Word is sufficient itself!

The Remarkable Triumph Described (Rev. 2:26-29)

The one who conquers and who keeps my works to the end: I will give him authority over the nations—"and he will rule them with an iron scepter; he will shatter them like pottery"—just as I have received this from my Father. Jesus' promise of authority over the nations speaks of the prominence and power given to believers in the millennial kingdom. He had already described this earlier in chapter 1 when He said He would make us "a kingdom, priests to his God and Father—to him be glory and dominion forever and ever. Amen" (v. 6). The promise of His firm rule had previously been revealed in Psalm 2:9; Isaiah 30:14; and Jeremiah 19:11.

The word **rule** in verse 27 is the Greek word reflecting the role of a pastor on several occasions. This indicates both the authority and the compassion with which that rule is to occur. Jesus was reminding the church that those faithful servants who labored there in Thyatira would one day be given great authority. This is consistent with the Lord's promise in Matthew 25:21: "Well done, good and faithful servant! You were faithful over a few things; I will put you in charge of many things. Share your master's joy."

Jesus essentially said to the church at Thyatira, "The problem is too severe for any of you to handle so I will not ask you to step in and do something about it. You just stay faithful. Stay away from the heresy. Don't buy into her lies or participate in her sinfulness. Keep yourselves pure from it and I will place you in authority over the nations."

An Exclusive Gospel

Peter spoke of the exclusiveness of the gospel while talking in front of the rulers, elders, scribes, and high priest in Jerusalem:

"There is salvation in no one else, for there is no other name under heaven given to people by which we must be saved" (Acts 4:12).

How can we best communicate to someone who is far from God that the gospel is for everyone, but it is the only way?

Who do you know who needs to hear the gospel message today?

Will you commit to pray for this person and look for opportunities to share the good news? If so, express that commitment to God now.

He went on to say of the conquering saints, **I will also give him the morning star.** This statement is referring to the presence of the Lord Himself in the lives of His believers throughout eternity. This is clearly explained in Revelation 22:16 where Jesus called Himself "the bright morning star." "The promise is then that the church at Thyatira, faithful to the calling of God, will eventually receive the morning star that is the abiding, close, imminent, and eternal fellowship with the Lord himself."[7]

"The morning star, of course, is none other than the Lord Jesus Himself. Possessing Him, we possess all."[7] What incredible power and privilege we will possess in heaven!

A CLOSER LOOK

Thyatira

Thyatira was the least important of all the seven cities yet it received the longest letter. Politically and religiously it had no great importance, but was a very important commercial city.

It was built in a broad valley, originally as a garrison of soldiers to protect the city of Pergamum. The city was poorly located for that purpose and unable to defend itself. Thus it was often destroyed by enemies and just as often was in the process of being rebuilt. When the enemy would come to attack the cities of Asia, Pergamum, being a fortified city, wanted to have some warning and thus set a garrison at the place that became Thyatira. If the enemy came, the soldiers would fight them at Thyatira and send word back to Pergamum that an enemy was approaching. The city was a diversion to protect citizens further up the valley.

Thus, Thyatira was wiped out quite frequently and often had to be restored. Its greatest significance was its trade guilds or unions. Lydia, the first convert in Macedonia was a seller of purple cloth from Thyatira (see Acts 16:14). Historically we know very little about Thyatira.

Personal Reflection

1. Read Revelation 2:19 regarding the works of the church at Thyatira. Which of these works do you find most prevalent in your own life? Which is most lacking? Explain.

2. Jesus commended this church because "your last works are greater than the first" (v. 19). What works of faith in your life are greater or stronger now than they were in the past? Explain.

3. The writer observes that "with all its good qualities, the church in Thyatira was radically deficient in holiness." Jesus exclaimed, "I am the one who examines minds and hearts" (v. 23). Which of the following best describes what Jesus would find in examining your mind and heart? My mind and heart are:

___ always focused on holiness;
___ often prompted to holiness;
___ sometimes stirred by thoughts of holiness;
___ rarely concerned with issues of holiness.

4. The One who examines hearts and minds also said, "I will give to each of you according to your works" (v. 23). Knowing that He sees both your works and the motives in your heart for doing those works, how does His promise to give "according to your works" impact your evaluation of yourself? Explain.

1. John Stott, *What Christ Thinks of the Church* (London: Angus Hudson Ltd., 1990) 60.
2. John Phillips, *Exploring Revelation* (Chicago: Moody Press, 1974) 67.
3. Vance Havner, *Repent or Else* (New York: Fleming H. Revell, 1958) 56.
4. Ibid., 53.
5. Stott, 68.
6. Paige Patterson, *Revelation,* The New American Commentary, Volume 39 (Nashville: B&H, 2012) 118.
7. Phillips, 73.

SARDIS

REVELATION 3:1-6

Set in the fertile Hermus River valley, Sardis was the leading city in that major valley. The Greeks referred to it as the greatest of all cities. It was a city of great strength with a reputation as an unconquerable fortress. However, it was a city of the past, living on its reputation rather than its present reality.

The river Pactolus flowed through the city and gold dust was a pleasant surprise to the inhabitants. This further made Sardis one of the wealthiest cities in Asia Minor. It was the most strategic area for agriculture among all the valleys of Asia Minor. Situated beneath the Acropolis, which was built on the peak of Mount Tmolus, its name was synonymous with wealth.

Jesus introduced Himself as **the one who has the seven spirits of God and the seven stars.** This refers to His omniscience and points out the completeness and power of God through His Holy Spirit. The seven stars are the angels, or messengers, of the church, and they are held in the hand of the Savior. **The seven Spirits of God** describes the fullness of the power and wisdom of the Holy Spirit. The character of the church at Sardis was well known to the One who has both the Holy Spirit and the seven stars.

This letter has no good word for the church at Sardis. Usually there was commendation and condemnation. Here there is no commendation. Even their **works** were described as being **dead**.

A False Reputation (Rev. 3:1)

The reputation of the church is immediately addressed. No wasted words here. The Lord got straight to the heart of the matter: **You have a reputation for**

being alive, but you are dead. Our Lord carefully observes and evaluates every church. His judgment is precise and accurate. He is the One to whom all churches are accountable. Sardis was an appealing church, a flourishing church from all outward standards. There did not seem to be anything lacking. It was a beehive of activity. The church program was functioning well.

There was no indication that heresy existed in the church at Sardis. There was no evidence of the presence of false teaching or false teachers. Heresy is evidence that a church has at least tried to find the truth. There was no searching for the truth at Sardis. The church was undisturbed by heresy.

They were also untroubled by persecutions from outside opposition. There were no pagan attacks or Jewish slander to face in Sardis. Sadly, the church at Sardis was lifeless and not worth attacking! A true church where the power of the Holy Spirit is active will always be under attack. Such a church is always politically incorrect and a thorn in the side of a godless culture. But this was not a problem in Sardis.

Sardis was a wealthy city and the church had no shortage of money. It was busy with many activities and had sufficient means to do them with excellence. In one swift sentence, the Lord destroyed the popular reputation of the church and revealed its spiritual bankruptcy. When Jesus examined this church, He declared, **You have a reputation for being alive, but you are dead.**

Other churches spoke well of this church. The surrounding community was amazed at the energy in its activities. But the Lord's careful analysis and precise observation revealed that it was all show and no substance. "There was form, but no force. It was 'faultily faultless, icily regular, splendidly null.'"[1]

Left: Columns of the Temple of Artemis at Sardis. The temple dates from 300 BC.

ILLUSTRATOR PHOTO/ BOB SCHATZ (11/34/5)

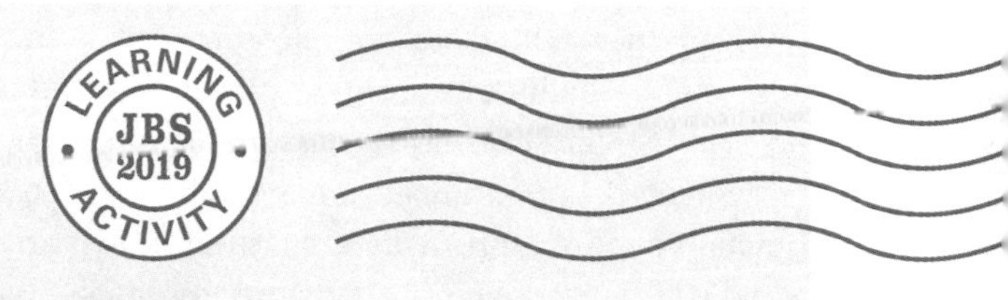

Mistaken Activity

"Write to the angel of the church in Sardis: Thus says the one who has the seven spirits of God and the seven stars: I know your works; you have a reputation for being alive, but you are dead" (Rev. 3:1).

"What a description: here was a spiritually dead corpse going through the motions of life. The church had mistaken activity for spirituality."

What might be evidence of a church that has mistaken activity for spirituality?

How can we guard against mistaking "activity for spirituality" in our personal lives?

In the life of our church?

This was not the opinion of others, but it was the strong evaluation of the Lord Himself. He is the One who walks among the churches and holds the pastors in His hands. This declaration is determined by the Spirit of God.

What a description: here was a spiritually dead corpse going through the motions of life. The church had mistaken activity for spirituality. It had deviated from the holy character that should have characterized the church. It had forgotten the assignment the Lord had given it to reach the world with the gospel. There were energetic activities, complex programs, and celebrations, but all were done without the reality of the Holy Spirit in the church. There was lots of smoke, but no fire! The very life and spiritual value of the church was gone.

"Outward appearances are notoriously deceptive; and this socially distinguished congregation was a spiritual graveyard."[2] It was not what it appeared to be. Our Lord Jesus Christ is not impressed with the pretenses we make, the activities we engage in, the promises we make, or even the apparent fulfillment of those promises.

Recall the words of God to Samuel as he sought the identity of the next king of Israel: "Do not look at his appearance or his stature because I have rejected him. Humans do not see what the LORD sees, for humans see what is visible, but the LORD sees the heart" (1 Sam. 16:7). The Lord Jesus carefully examines the heart. He not only knows what we do, but why we do it. He knows how genuine our faith is and if we are genuine behind the mask that we put up for others to see. What a tragedy when a church is dead and does not even know it!

A living church will be a growing church. Now that means far more than numerical growth. Growth is not simply defined by numbers. There are many kinds of growth and each kind is vitally important. There will be growth in faith, in ministry, in witness, and in mission. There will be growth in compassion and in the depth of our walk with the Lord. The law of life is the very opposite of stagnation. A living church is a growing church.

A living church will have compassion for each other and for the lost. It will have unity. Division and schism are signs of decay and death. When a physical body begins to die, normally the various organs of the body cease to function together. The body dies through the disintegration of the unity of the body. A living church, in which the Spirit of God lives and guides, is a church united on the things of God and on the mission and purpose of the church.

A living church has deep emotion. There is nothing wrong with that. Don't be afraid to feel your faith. I weep, I sing, I laugh, I mourn. Those are signs of life. Only the dead have no tears, laughter, music, or sorrow. That is all part of life. There is emotion in life and should characterize the church.

The signs of a dead church relate to their refusal to leave the past behind. When a church lives in the past, focused on its reputation and history, that church is dead. When a church is more concerned for form than life, for ritual than heart, it is dead. When members are more concerned about church activities than we are about the glory of God, the church is dead. When a church loves systems more than Jesus and more than it loves people, it is dead. When a church is more focused on material things than spiritual things, it is dead. A church is either growing, living, or it is dying.

If a church is dead, its people are dead since we are the church. The church is dead in the sense that the presence of the Lord is gone and its many activities lack life and energy. Everyone of us in the church must examine our hearts in light of this message to the church at Sardis.

Jesus went on in Revelation 3:2 to say, "I have not found your works complete before my God." This church had not met the high standard expected by the living Lord. As Jesus examined this church He declared that their works never fulfilled the purpose that God intended. What a sad thing for the church! They sang, prayed, and praised but never really glorified God. Their works were incomplete.

The description of the remnant of faithful believers gives us an insight into what kind of death Jesus was speaking of. It is said of them that they have not defiled or soiled their clothes (v. 4). "So this death was defilement. Sin had seeped into the church ... beneath the pious exterior of that respectable congregation was secret uncleanness."[3] Apparently this condition had spread unnoticed throughout the fiber of the church.

Being a Christian is not a way of doing certain things, it is a certain way of doing everything. Here was a church that was persistent in tireless activities, did all the right things, had a great reputation; but the Great Physician said, "You are dead!" Our Lord demands that a church must have more than a reputation of life, but must possess true life. Sardis was well described in Isaiah when the Lord said of Israel, "These people approach me with their speeches to honor me with lip-service—yet their hearts are far from me, and human rules direct their worship of me" (Isa. 29:13).

A Specific Remedy (Rev. 3:2-3)

The remedy for the church was to **be alert and strengthen what remains, which is about to die ... remember, then, what you have received and heard; keep it, and repent.**

Five demanding commands follow like the sound of a machine gun: **Be alert ... strengthen ... remember ... keep it ... repent.** God is always in the process of calling the church to actions. Impregnable Sardis had been conquered twice because its watchman had not been alert. The things God has given us must not be taken for granted. One never drifts anywhere worth going. We always drift away from God into sin and rebellion. We never drift into obedience and Christlikeness. So the Lord told the believers at Sardis to wake up and be alert.

His commands are clear. He is eager to put life into dry bones. The Lord did not tell them to stop doing what they were doing, but to fill what they were doing with true devotion to God. What they were doing was not wrong. They needed to be doing them filled with power. The things that remained were what the church was created to do. Those things would include praying, preaching, teaching, ministering, and witnessing.

Don't abandon those things but strengthen them. Don't abandon the activities of the church, but breathe life into them. Make those activities expressions of love for Christ and for God. Those are the things **which [are] about to die.** Ceremony and form without heart for God will die, and the people will die with them. Put life into them and God will bless it.

Jesus said that He had not found their works **complete before my God.** Do we dare to look into the face of God and ask if our works are complete before Him? Or do we just have a name without the reality, a reputation with no heart to live for Him? When external things lack internal force, they will decay and crumble.

Remember, then, what you have received and heard; keep it, and repent. *Remember* and *repent* are both imperatives. This is the Lord's command to the church. This church was drifting with the culture, active for God, but betraying the God it claimed to serve. Christ was calling for decisive action on the part of believers in Sardis.

The Lord included **what you have received** as part of that which needed to be strengthened. What had they received? Obviously they had received the gospel. But is that all? No, because even biblical orthodoxy can become dead orthodoxy. What keeps a church alive is not just the gospel message, but the presence of the Holy Spirit.

He is the One whom they had received. That is the greatest gift for the believer—the Spirit of God Himself. He is the One who transforms our lives and fills us with all the fruit of the Spirit. He is the One who brings love, joy, and peace into our lives through His grace. This church had developed a system that did not require the Holy Spirit. What a sad day in Sardis!

It is when the first movement of God in a church is forgotten that a church begins to die. The Sardis believers previously had been living lost in darkness and God brought the glorious light of salvation to them. They had once lived in untruth, then they knew the truth. Every church was born with the blessing of

God upon it. That is how churches begin. When that blessing becomes institutionalized and the presence of God becomes the patronage of men, death begins to set into a church.

The church at Sardis had forgotten why they were a church. Church is not about us, about our needs, preferences, likes, or dislikes. When we focus on ourselves and our comfort and concerns, we dishonor the Lord Jesus Christ. Church is about Him. Outward activities do not guarantee inward vitality.

A stern warning ensued from the Lord: **Remember, then, what you have received and heard; keep it, and repent. If you are not alert, I will come like a thief, and you have no idea at what hour I will come upon you.** This is a clear warning that Sardis was not ready for His return. I wonder if our churches are ready for His return! In Sardis, outwardly they looked alive, but inwardly they were dead.

The Lord Jesus Christ was calling the church to a painful self-evaluation and self-judgment. The newness of their salvation had now become routine. They became accustomed to lifeless activities. "The movement becomes a monument."[4] The response must be to repent and return to the vibrant faith of their beginning as a church. **Remember, then, what you have received and heard; keep it, and repent.**

Reputation and reality do not always coincide. What the world sees is not the same as what God sees. While we live in a world that is always placing demands upon us, we need to be reminded that we are ultimately and primarily accountable to God. It is before Him that we will stand and to Him that we will give account.

The warning for failure to repent is clear. Without repentance and a return to what they embraced at the beginning, the Lord would suddenly confront the church at Sardis with its false reputation and would remove its lampstand. He would come against the church and would destroy that reputation. He promised the church at Ephesus, "I will come to you and remove your lampstand from its place, unless you repent" (2:5). Here He repeated that warning to repent with even stronger commands.

A Faithful Remnant (Rev. 3:4-6)

There was a bright spot, even in Sardis, even among the ungodly. In the midst of a culture of worldliness in the church, there was a fresh breeze of life from the Holy Spirit present. The Master's Minority was there. The Lord Jesus spotlighted this faithful group of believers who had **not defiled their clothes** and who **will walk with me in white, because they are worthy.** Their worthiness is not their own righteousness, but that of the worthy One who sacrificed His life for our sins, and in whose righteousness we now stand.

Of the ones who are worthy, the Lord further stated, **I will never erase his name from the book of life but will acknowledge his name before my Father and before his angels.** This is not a suggestion that some believers may have their names erased from the book of life. It is simply a promise for all true believers of their security in Christ. There is nothing here or anywhere in the Bible that indicates that salvation can be withdrawn from one who has received it.

God always has a remnant of faithful believers. Even in Sardis there was a remnant of righteous believers who remained faithful, and the Lord was pleased. That godly remnant lived among those who compromised. Even though they were in a difficult place in the culture and in the church, they remained faithful. These worthy believers would walk with Him in glory.

What a day that will be! The Lord Himself will lead us into God's throne room. We will hear Him call our name and Jesus will present us as His cherished and beloved. We will be dressed in the brilliance of white like Jesus wore on the mount of transfiguration (Matt. 17:2). What a reward for faithful believers!

Our faith will always run counter to the society around us, and sometimes even within the church environment. As we are seeing in America today, we are in the minority. To stand for Christ and for biblical principles is to be labeled a bigot, hateful, angry, and a host of things even worse. We need to remember that the battle is not ours but the Lord's, and He will be with us every step of our earthly journey.

To those who persevere and who are victors will be given white clothes and they will never have their names taken from the book of life. The Lord will acknowledge them and claim them as His own before God and His angels. Those who appear before the great white throne judgment will have their names searched for in the book of life. But from the Lamb's book of life there will be no deletions.

What a wonderful message of security. One of the most beautiful and significant expressions in God's Word appears in the closing verses of this letter: **I ... will acknowledge his name before my Father and before his angels.** When we arrive in heaven, the Lord Himself will take us by the hand, usher us through the gate and past the angels, past the redeemed already there, and bring us to the very throne of God. There He will confess us before the Father, that our names are synonymous with His.

Here is an incredible picture. The victors or overcomers will be clothed in the bright white holiness of the Lord Himself and will walk as worthy with the angels in the very presence of the Lord God. He listens carefully as the Lord Jesus Christ claims his name for all the world to hear: "This is my ransomed one who is cherished and treasured and is with Me!"

Jesus' final words to the church at Sardis are the same as to the other churches. **Let anyone who has ears to hear listen to what the Spirit says to the churches.**

A CLOSER LOOK

Sardis

Sardis had served as the capital of Lydian King Croesus and was the recipient of his vast gold treasure. It was the first city to mint coins in silver and gold. The temple of Artemis there was much smaller than the Artemision in Ephesus, but it was exquisitely and expensively adorned. Sardis also served as a district judicial center for Rome.

Sardis was awarded the title "temple warden" three times in the second century when all the cities of the Roman Province of Asia competed for the honor of building temples to the Roman Emperor. Christians grew strong there in spite of much opposition and a wicked culture.

Historically the city had been conquered twice through the carelessness of its sentinels. Only one avenue gave a smooth approach to the city and was easily defended even though its ascent was steep. Other avenues to the city faced vertical walls virtually impossible to scale. No one could conquer the city by scaling the walls unless the guards did not do their jobs. Twice the city was conquered through lack of vigilance and carelessness by those who were assigned to protect the city.

Heart Check

Revelation 3:1-6 is not the only place the Bible talks about looking past the external appearances and seeing a person's heart attitudes. Read the following verses. For each, identify to whom God was speaking and summarize His message in that situation.

1 Samuel 16:7

Matthew 23:27

What are the attitudes God wants to see when He looks at our hearts?

Personal Reflection

1. Sardis was "a city of the past, living on its reputation rather than its present reality." Spiritually, are you ever guilty of living on past reputation rather than present reality? Are you currently living in the past or present? Explain.

2. The church at Sardis had "a reputation for being alive, but [it was] dead" (v. 1). How do we tell if we are spiritually alive or dead?

3. Read Revelation 3:2-3. Explain in your own words how, according to these verses, a person living on past reputation can remedy that situation.

4. What does it mean to you that for "the one who conquers," Jesus "will acknowledge his name before my Father and before his angels" (v. 5)?

1. Vance Havner, *Repent or Else* (New York: Fleming H. Revell, 1958) 63.

2. John Stott, *What Christ Thinks of the Church* (London: Angus Hudson Ltd., 1990) 78.

3. Ibid., 79.

4. John Phillips, *Exploring Revelation* (Chicago: Moody Press, 1974) 77.

PHILADELPHIA

REVELATION 3:7-13

Philadelphia was one of the newest of the cities in Asia Minor, certainly the youngest of the seven cities in Revelation 2–3. Resting impressively about 700 feet above sea level on a large plateau on the slopes of Mount Tmolus, it overlooked a fertile valley enriched by the volcanic ash deposited there. The city was founded in the second century BC by Attalus, king of Pergamum, to honor his loyalty to his brother, Eumenes II, whom he had succeeded as king. The name itself was fitting as it means *brotherly love.* It was located on the Imperial Post Road which came from Rome, through Troas, Pergamum, and Sardis, and on further to the east. The road was the main line of communication for the emperor in Rome to points east.

Philadelphia quickly became a very important and wealthy trade center for Asia Minor and beyond. But the region was subject to frequent earthquakes. Indeed, during the reign of Emperor Tiberius, a major quake destroyed the city (AD 17), forcing it to rebuild.

The Lord had no condemnation for this city. His promise to the church there was that He would make the overcomers "a pillar in the temple of my God" (3:12). Because the city's many architectural pillars were weakened by the recurring earthquakes, the promise that Jesus would make them pillars in God's sanctuary would be something they could quickly visualize.

This was a favored church of our Lord. Jesus loved the church and spoke tenderly of His love for it in this letter (see v. 9). He presented Himself to this faithful church with three strong descriptive phrases: **the Holy One, the true one, the one who has the key of David.** Jesus is the Holy One. The name that was ascribed to God the Father in the Old Testament is now given to the Lord Jesus Christ. "He has that quality of being which belongs to Him alone,"[1] which men can never have by themselves.

Above: The remains of a Roman arch with later construction on top. Possibly an old city gate or major street gate in ancient Philadelphia.

ILLUSTRATOR PHOTO/ BOB SCHATZ (11/30/5)

He called Himself **the true one.** The specific word chosen for "true" means someone or something that is real or genuine and not artificial or deceptive. Authentic blessing and satisfaction is to be found in Him.

He also described Himself as having the **key of David,** indicating that He is the rightful heir to David's throne and has access to the throne, with legal right by inheritance as the sole heir to the throne. His is the absolute authority which is beyond challenge. He is "the way, the truth, and the life. No one come to the Father except through" Him (John 14:6). Access to the Father is through Jesus Christ alone!

The further description reveals Him opening wide a door that no person can close, and closing a door that no person can open. This speaks of His omnipotence. Simply put, we had better listen to Him! The obvious conclusion is that when God opens a door, we can and must go through it!

The church at Philadelphia was in revival. It had survived the test. After having been tried, it was found to be true. It was having an evangelistic revival, for it had a vision of reaching the world for Christ. It had an ecclesiastical revival because its watchword was the blessed return of our Lord.

Jesus loved this church, and everything He said to them speaks of His special love and concern for them.

The Open Door (Rev. 3:8)

This is a powerful verse with many important issues. It is not just referring to any **open door**. It is a door which He Himself has opened for the church and it is His gift to the church, carrying with it a tremendous privilege. This open door concept has been expressed before. The apostle Paul said, "A wide door for effective ministry has opened for me—yet many oppose me" (1 Cor. 16:9). Where there is opportunity, there is always opposition.

Later Paul would remark, "When I came to Troas to preach the gospel of Christ, ... the Lord opened a door for me" (2 Cor. 2:12). And to the Colossians he asked that they "pray also for us that God may open a door to us for the word, to speak the mystery of Christ" (Col. 4:3).

That open door was the right to preach the gospel, to evangelize the world. We have an opportunity to preach the gospel to the world today, but that door might not remain open much longer. In every age, the door of opportunity for proclamation of the gospel is opened. It will remain open till God shuts it!

God opens doors, and prompt obedience leads us to grasp an opportunity that will soon be gone. Doors are being opened and closed around the world today. We must enter the open doors the Lord places before us while they are open.

The city of Philadelphia had been established to promote Greek culture, language, and worship. It had succeeded in a great way in that task. Now the church of Philadelphia was commissioned to take the gospel of Jesus Christ to the same areas where the city had spread the cultural characteristics of Greece.

Jesus said, **You have but little power.** The believers were extremely weak! That seems a little strange. The door is open but you have limited strength. Members in Philadelphia had little wealth, status, or prestige. They were a small group of people, in the minority. So Jesus praised them for their weakness rather than for their strength.

He did not praise them because they were strong and able to do great things. He praised them because they were weak and they knew it. They would have to rely on Him! They would learn, as the apostle Paul did, "I will most gladly boast all the more about my weaknesses, so that Christ's power may reside in me" (2 Cor. 12:9).

This church was under tremendous pressure, persecution, and opposition. They were a weak, small church, but with a big faith. They had been faithful to the things of God. They had **kept my word and have not denied my name.** Both *kept* and *denied* are in the aorist tense, which refers to a specific occurrence in the past that still stands true. The clear implication is that there was a specific

Open Doors

"Look, I have placed before you an open door ..." (Rev. 3:8).

"That open door was the right to preach the gospel, to evangelize the world. ... God opens doors, and prompt obedience leads us to grasp an opportunity that will soon be gone. Doors are being opened and closed around the world today. We must enter the open doors the Lord places before us while they are open."

What open door has God placed before you as an individual believer?

What open door has God placed before us as a church today?

What kinds of things might prevent us from stepping through the open doors God places before us?

Pray for discerning eyes to see the open doors and for God's strength to step through those doors in prompt obedience.

time in the past when the church faced severe trials and attacks, yet they stood strong and emerged victorious.

They were weak in physical things, but like the rock of Gibraltar in their faith and courage. They held tightly to the Word of the Lord and did not betray their devotion to Him. Because they had "kept" His word, He would "keep" them (Rev. 3:10).

William Barclay suggests that the literal translation of "my command to endure" (v. 10) is "the word of my endurance."[2] Christ's endurance is the model for believers' endurance. That is our motivation. We live looking unto Him who endured the cross and despised the shame (see Heb. 12:1-2). He is our example and also the guarantor of our endurance. In Him we endure!

The Philadelphia believers were strong in their loyalty to the Lord and to the Word of God. Satan strives to corrupt the Word of God. Some critics subtract from it, while others add to it. This church kept their faith in the Word of God and **[had] not denied my name**, and were commended for it by the Lord Himself.

Supernatural Deliverance (Rev. 3:9-10)

Like the church at Smyrna, this church at Philadelphia was under merciless siege from the Jewish community. Jesus again spoke of these attacks as coming from those **from the synagogue of Satan, who claim to be Jews and are not, but are lying.** As in Smyrna, these false Jews impugned the character of the Christians and lied about them. This angry opposition surely tempted the church to remain uninvolved in reaching the lost. Some must have refused to stir up trouble with the Jewish community by the faithful proclamation of the gospel.

It is interesting that the two churches for whom the Lord had no condemnation were the two situated in the very home of Satan. Even when confronted with violent and slanderous opposition, they stood strong. Adversity could not prevent this church from its mission. The Lord said the church had kept His command to endure (v. 8). It was in this city of violent resistance that the Lord opened up a wide door of opportunity to proclaim the gospel of salvation.

What an inspiration and encouragement this is for us today. In a world rapidly racing toward spiritual destruction, we have been given the opportunity to stand true to the Word of God and to our Savior Jesus Christ. Satanic opposition cannot stop the faithful church (see Matt. 16:18).

I will also keep you from the hour of testing that is going to come on the whole world to test those who live on the earth. This **hour of testing** is that severe persecution that was building against the church. The storm was approaching but the Lord promised He would **keep you from the hour of testing.** Whatever tribulation came, Christ would walk through it with them, sustain them, and keep Satan from being unleashed upon them. He has promised to walk with all of us in every moment of our journey in this life.

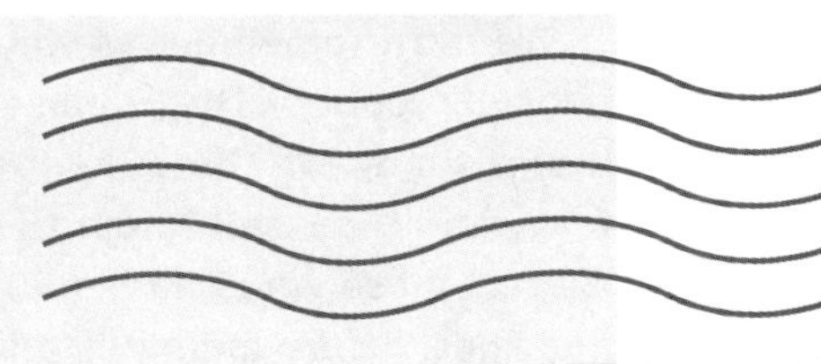

Counterculture Ideas

Many of the things that Jesus taught about God's kingdom run counter to the popular ideas of the culture. Here are just a few of those countercultural ideas:

- *"Blessed are the humble, for they will inherit the earth." – Matthew 5:5*
- *"For whoever wants to save his life will lose it, but whoever loses his life because of me will find it." – Matthew 16:25*
- *"But many who are first will be last, and the last first." – Matthew 19:30*

Here in the words spoken to the church at Philadelphia, we find yet another countercultural idea. In Revelation 3:8, Jesus complimented the church in Philadelphia for their weakness.

How is weakness commonly viewed in our culture today?

"Jesus said, 'You have but little power.' The believers were extremely weak! That seems a little strange. The door is open but you have limited strength. Members in Philadelphia had little wealth, status, or prestige. They were a small group of people, in the minority. So Jesus praised them for their weakness rather than their strength."

As believers, how can weakness be a strength?

We must remember as we look closely at this letter that we are studying a book of prophecy. The promise of the Lord to these persecuted saints was, **I will make them [of the synagogue of Satan] come and bow down at your feet, and they will know that I have loved you.** Here is the incredible promise that those who had persecuted, slandered, and attacked them would come and kneel before them. Historically that has not yet occurred, so we must see it as awaiting fulfillment in the millennial kingdom.

This is a reminder that God is still in control of history and of all the events that includes. He is still moving the moments of time toward the glorious conclusion of His return to the earth and the establishment of His kingdom. He will protect them in the **hour of testing**. This is another indication that He is in control of the events of time and eternity. The church at Philadelphia had kept His word; now He pledged to keep them from the testing to come.

Certainly, there was comfort for those struggling believers in Philadelphia with the current and approaching persecution. These words would have been an affirmation of the very presence and power of the Lord for them through whatever lay ahead. That is also a promise we can claim. Nothing can come into our lives that does not go through the hands of our Lord, and He is with us every step of the journey. Praise God for that and for the promise of future fulfillment when we reign with Him in His Kingdom.

The Lord's Promised Return (Rev. 3:11-13)

Next the Lord spoke to the church about His promised return: **I am coming soon. Hold on to what you have, so that no one takes your crown.** The church that fulfills its calling will live in a constant awareness of the imminence of His return. The **crown** promised to these faithful saints is not their salvation. This does not imply that someone can take their salvation away. The crown is our reward that we receive from the Lord.

We are saved by faith, but we are rewarded according to works. Our faithful service with the Lord will accrue for us rewards that we will receive in heaven. Perhaps these are the crowns that we will lay before the throne of God as the twenty-four elders did in 4:10. Every believer and church should live with the constant expectation of the return of our Lord.

The Lord's promise is, **I am coming soon.** This is doubtless an expression of the certainty of His coming. The certainty of His coming does not indicate the timing of the Lord's return. The church must continually keep the possibility of an immediate second coming in view as it ministers. Knowing that it could be at any time, the expectation of His return is the ingredient of our faith that keeps us aggressively and passionately proclaiming the gospel.

Jesus spoke of this in His parable of the wicked servant in Matthew 24:48-51. Recall that the wicked servant took advantage of the absence of the master to conduct himself in a manner in which the master would not approve. The sudden return of the master brought judgment upon the disobedient servant.

The apostle Paul warned the Thessalonians of the inevitable judgment that is coming to the disobedient and unbelievers when the Lord returns (see 2 Thess. 1:5-10). When He comes again, He will take decisive, final, and permanent action to deliver justice.

Simon Peter warned his readers that those living in reckless evil behavior "will give an account to the one who stands ready to judge the living and the dead" (1 Pet. 4:5).

Throughout the New Testament the message to the church is the same. Don't get careless and abandon your strong faith in the Lord, because you do not know the time of His return. We all should live in the awareness of His soon return!

Because of His imminent return, Jesus told the Philadelphian church, **Hold on to what you have, so that no one takes your crown.** There are so many things that could steal our crowns: cold hearts, worldliness, prayerlessness, discouragement, heresy, friends, and sometimes even our families. Both success and failure will seek to take our crowns.

Jesus challenges us to hold tight what we have received so we don't let anyone or anything steal our crown. That crown is the crown of a victorious athlete in competitive games. This is the *stefanos* crown of the victor, and the admonition is to not forfeit our crown by disobedience. No one can take our crown, but we can forfeit it by compromise.

When He returns, there will be stability and security in Him. To the conqueror He promised, **I will make [that one] a pillar in the temple of my God, and he will never go out again.** In that city of massive earthquakes and crumbling pillars across its terrain, this promise would convey a vivid picture in the hearts of victorious believers—no more instability as was common in Philadelphia. The conquerors would be made pillars in the New Jerusalem which will come down from heaven. They would never have to face the need to flee from earthquakes again.

The day is coming when the uncertainty and peril present in Philadelphia would be replaced by the consistency and permanence of all believers. They would never again have to endure the transient nature of the things they experienced in Philadelphia.

Furthermore, the Lord would **write on him the name of my God and the name of the city of my God—the new Jerusalem, which comes down out of heaven from my God—and my new name.** The last chapter of Revelation declares, "There will no longer be any curse. The throne of God and of the Lamb will be in the city, and his servants will worship him. They will see his face, and his name will be on their foreheads" (Rev. 22:3-4).

The overcomers in Philadelphia would be permanently identified with the new Jerusalem. Wherever believers in the millennial kingdom may go in this entire universe, that name immediately introduces them as belonging to the new Jerusalem.

Believers will be identified with the **new name** of the Lord Himself. That new name will be more meaningful and more glorious than we now know. The extent of that name has not yet been revealed in this present age. But in eternity we shall bear His new name forever!

Taking a new name was something very familiar to the citizens of Philadelphia. Because it was one of the cities on the plain, it was often known as Decapolis. After the devastation of the earthquake in AD 17, the Roman Emperor, Tiberius, assisted the city of Philadelphia in many ways. He removed them from taxation by Rome and made a generous gift to rebuild the city. In response to his kindness to them, the citizens of Philadelphia renamed their city Neocaesarea (or New Caesar), and under a similar action by Vespasian later they renamed their city Flavia, after the family name of Vespasian.[3]

To the victorious in Philadelphia, Jesus Christ would give a new name known to no mortal man. But in the age to come when Christ has established His kingdom, those conquering believers will bear His new name which declares that they belong to Him and are participants in His ultimate victory.

The name of the Lord represents the right to have authority in the kingdom to come. That name on our foreheads entitles us to entrance into the city of God. It entitles us to participate in the service and worship of our eternal God. It is our stamp of citizenship. That name of Jesus Christ is our security of eternity.

A CLOSER LOOK

Philadelphia

Philadelphia was about 28 miles southeast of Sardis, 43 miles from Laodicea, and 65 miles from Smyrna. It sat in the center of the seven churches. It was sometimes called "little Athens" because of the magnificent temples and public buildings there. Like the other churches in Asia Minor, there was a strong Jewish population in the city with their own synagogue. It was a border town, built on the border between Mysia, Lydia, and Phrygia.

Volcanic cliffs outside the city were called inkwells and were a constant reminder of the volcanic activity in the region. Sitting on the Anatolian fault line, it was subject to frequent and violent earthquakes. No city suffered more from earthquakes than Philadelphia. The constant earthquakes made it difficult to determine a population for the city at the end of the first century. Most of the inhabitants would leave the city when the quakes would come. Since they farmed the fertile valley, they would live in tents until the city seemed safe to reenter. The frequent quakes caused many cracks in the walls and buildings of the city. The ancients often remarked that the city walls were unsafe.

Personal Reflection

1. The church at Philadelphia is one of only two churches in Revelation 2–3 to whom Jesus offered no criticism. Review 3:7-13 and suggest why you think that might be.

2. Jesus placed an "open door" (v. 8) for ministry before the church at Philadelphia. Describe a time He placed an open door for ministry before you.

3. Explain how having "little power" (v. 8) is good.

1. William Barclay, *The Revelation of John*, Revised Edition (Philadelphia: Westminster Press, 1976) 127.
2. Ibid., 131.
3. Ibid., 126.

LAODICEA

REVELATION 3:14-22

Resting on a narrow hill just south of the Lycus River, the city of Laodicea had a unique history. At first it was not a place of any significance, but it quickly became a very prosperous city.

Many of the residents were Jews, and very early in the Christian era it became a very important center for Christianity. An aqueduct began at Baspinar Spring near Denizli and brought the water into the valley and back up into the city with large carved stone pipes. The aqueduct seems to have been destroyed by an earthquake. The remaining arches lean to one side but are not broken.

There was a unique stadium still well-preserved near the southern edge of the city. The seats were located on two sides of a narrow valley. The stadium was closed in at both ends. The stadium was circular with the total complex being about 300 yards long. Used primarily for running, the length of the track was about 200 yards or one *stadia* long.

In the earthquake-prone region, the city often experienced the effects of the tremors. After the AD 60 earthquake destroyed the city, it was rebuilt by the citizens with no help from Rome, so great was its wealth. This prosperity doubtless contributed to the "lukewarm" status of the church. Smyrna and Laodicea, the two churches most wealthy and comfortable, were the churches most rebuked of the seven churches. The five churches most persecuted and oppressed were the ones most commended. The Laodicean church flourished but had no passionate love for the Lord. It was, instead, lukewarm.

It was to this lifeless, indifferent, cool church that Jesus addressed His last letter and spoke as the **originator of God's creation,** the infinite energy that animated all life. We are now at the last of these seven letters and the one with the most severe condemnation.

We are looking at the church most like contemporary churches in America. What we understand in this message is true about ourselves and our contemporary world. Reading this letter is like looking into a mirror and seeing our own face—our own time. The church in America, generally speaking, is weak and anemic. We are nominal in our faith and faulty in our worship. We are definitely living in the spirit of the Laodicean age.

Laodicea means "the rule of the people." It describes a time and place when the church was enamored with its own interests and preferences. It was a time when the Word of God was ignored and the desires of the people were magnified. The church judged itself by standards of its own choosing. Sadly, this is characteristic of much church life today.

Jesus had nothing good to say about this church. There is no commendation. Even when He spoke of those whom he loved (see v. 19), the word *love* is not *agape*, it is *phileo*. *Agape* is a Godly, self-sacrificing kind of love. *Phileo* is a love that is more casual and less intense, requiring less sacrifice. This church had been so rebellious against God that His rebuke was given out of affection rather than intensive love.

Below: Roman arches in buildings at ancient Laodicea.

ILLUSTRATOR PHOTO/ BOB SCHATZ (11/31/10)

The Lord presented Himself as **The Amen, the faithful and true witness, the originator of God's creation. Amen** is the last word one can say. When everything else has been said, the only thing left to say is amen. It is a word of finality, certainty, and authority. Jesus reveals and establishes God's promises. He is the final word, the absolute truth from God.

He is the **faithful and true witness.** Others may render false witness consistently, but He will always give a clear and truthful testimony. He is the One who keeps His word. He is the **originator**, the creator **of God's creation**. The Gospel of John says of Him, "All things were created through him, and apart from him not one thing was created that has been created" (John 1:3). Everything in creation indelibly bears His mark upon it. "He is the image of the invisible God, the firstborn over all creation. For everything was created by him, in heaven and on earth, the visible and the invisible, whether thrones or dominions or rulers or authorities—all things have been created through him and for him. He is before all things, and by him all things hold together" (Col. 1:15-17). Jesus was not created by God, but is the source and origin of all creation. He is the moving force of all creation and by Him everything consists or holds together.

Tragic Indifference (Rev. 3:15-16)

Jesus declared, **You are neither cold nor hot. I wish that you were cold or hot. So, because you are lukewarm, and neither hot nor cold, I am going to vomit you out of my mouth.** The worst possible condition anyone could be is lukewarm. It reveals a lack of passion, apathy, and indifference. Lukewarm means without enthusiasm. It describes total self-focus by an individual.

Vance Havner said, "The condition of the Laodicean church was nauseating. They were a little too cold to be hot and a little too hot to be cold, a little too bad to be good and a little too good to be bad. Cold water is not nauseating, neither is hot water, but lukewarm water is sickening."[1]

A lukewarm person lives in criticism without compassion, with no conviction of sin. Such individuals are more concerned about their own comfort and preferences than about worshiping God. They are completely self-centered, self-occupied, self-satisfied, self-sufficient, self-absorbed, and self-confident. Simply put, they have completely compromised the things of God.

The people in Laodicea would easily understand this very clearly. Laodicea had mineral springs where people would come to bathe for health purposes. Those springs had the taste of mineral content and were not hot or cold. If one tried to drink the water, it was nauseating. That is how Jesus described these people. They were nauseating to God! A lukewarm Christian is an oxymoron, a contradiction of terms. It is like saying dry water, cold heat, clean dirt. It just did not make sense.

Cold water was refreshing and life giving. Hot water had medicinal and healing capacity. The Lord would prefer either of those, but never the lukewarmness that was neither refreshing nor healing. G. Campbell Morgan said, "Lukewarmness is the worst form of blasphemy."[2]

They did not deny the gospel, they were just indifferent to it. They knew that sinners were lost, they just made no attempt to lead them to Christ. The cross was not denied, it was just ignored. Consequently, the Lord said, **I am going to vomit you out of my mouth.** The condition was intolerable. He was not speaking of removing the believers from their relationship with God, but with taking the lampstand out of the church and removing the opportunity for the church to be a bearer of light.

G. A. Studdert-Kennedy wrote an incisive poem called "When Jesus Came to Birmingham." It is a vivid description of the church at Laodicea, and of many churches today.

When Jesus came to Golgotha, they hanged Him on a tree,
They drove great nails through hands and feet, and made a Calvary;
They crowned Him with a crown of thorns, red were His wounds and deep,
For those were crude and cruel days, and human flesh was cheap.

When Jesus came to Birmingham, they simply passed Him by.
They would not hurt a hair of Him, they only let Him die;
For men had grown more tender, and they would not give Him pain,
They only just passed down the street, and left Him in the rain.

Still Jesus cried, 'Forgive them, for they know not what they do,'
And still it rained the winter rain that drenched Him through and through;
The crowds went home and left the streets without a soul to see,
And Jesus crouched against a wall, and cried for Calvary.

Such was the nauseating indifference that characterized the church at Laodicea as the Lord He resolved to vomit them out of His mouth.

Deluded Independence (Rev. 3:17)

For you say, "I'm rich; I have become wealthy and need nothing." The church was independent and arrogant. It was a silk-stocking town, a real-life success story, famous for its wool industry, and very wealthy. They had

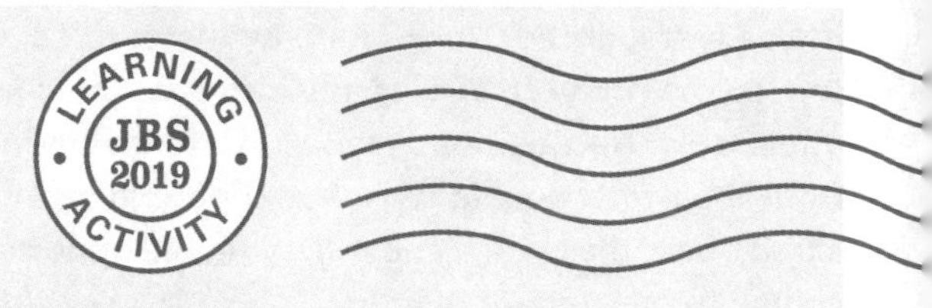

Indifference

"They did not deny the gospel, they were just indifferent to it. They knew that sinners were lost. They just made no attempt to lead them to Christ. The cross was not denied, it was just ignored."

Christ had strong words of condemnation for the church at Laodicea and their "lukewarmness"—neither hot nor cold.

If we are guilty of having a lukewarm faith, what might that look like ...

In our relationships with family members?

In our activity at church?

In our enthusiasm for sharing the gospel?

In our willingness to forgive?

everything they needed and were not interested in anyone else, even God.

Sounds like America today! We often have kicked God out of the public square so that He is not welcome in our schools, in our government, or anywhere in our society. Many are convinced we have all we need, and we don't need Him in our lives anymore.

Jesus continued to describe the true condition of the Laodicean believers: **You don't realize that you are wretched, pitiful, poor, blind, and naked.** This is a graphic picture of the difference between what a church thinks of itself and what the Lord knows the condition to be. What a wake-up call for Laodicea and for any church in any age!

Wretched is a unique word that is used only one other time in the New Testament. In Romans 7:24 the apostle Paul used the word to describe his own sinfulness. He said, "What a wretched man I am!" The word means "to be pressed with a burden." In Laodicea it is not the burden of poverty, it is the heavier burden of wealth.

The most dangerous place for any church or believer is when they think they have it all and don't need anything else. The real question is not whether the church can survive persecution. There are now more believers in China than in America, and they live under severe persecution. The church can survive persecution; it is uncertain if it can survive prosperity.

The word *pitiful* is surprising, as this church lived in a city known for its luxury and wealth. Yet this church was to be pitied. The word *poor* describes one who is without provisions, a pauper or beggar. Imagine, poverty in the midst of extravagant luxury. Rich in the earthly, but poverty-stricken in the eternal.

The word *blind* could better be translated "nearsighted." It describes those who have no vision and no discernment. This church was clueless of its true condition. Laodicea was famous for the development of eye salves from the mineral waters. Its development of ocular treatments was far ahead of any other city in the ancient world. Yet spiritually, they had no vision.

The word *naked* described a church lacking in the covering of the glory and majesty of God. It speaks of a church whose very character was exposed before God and the world. Here was a church that possessed none of the covering the bride of Christ should possess and no ability to be the witness for Christ it was established to be. Other churches had "white clothes" (Rev. 3:4-5). This church had nothing.

Genuine Wealth (Rev. 3:18-19)

In spite of the repulsive condition that was nauseating to the Lord, He took time to give strong counsel to the church. He told them how to get out of their lethargy

Surviving Prosperity

"The church can survive persecution; it is uncertain if it can survive prosperity."

Prosperity sounds like a good thing. So why/when is prosperity a danger for the church?

In what ways might believers struggle with prosperity?

For a believer, what's the proper attitude toward prosperity?

and indifference: **I advise you to buy from me gold refined in the fire so that you may be rich, white clothes so that you may be dressed and your shameful nakedness not be exposed, and ointment to spread on your eyes so that you may see.**

The importance of this purchase is that it is **from me.** This is gold that is "refined in the fire" and cannot be found anywhere else. The Lord Jesus told them to secure from Him **gold refined in the fire.** This gold represents authentic riches. This gold is subjected to extreme heat so that all the impurities can be removed. The impurities rise to the top in the heat and what remains is the purest gold. This spiritual gold can only be received from the Lord Himself.

The price of the gold is not mentioned, but surely it involved repentance, faith, and submission to the Lord. This is not speaking of purchasing salvation, as that was accomplished by Christ's death on the cross. Playing upon the commercial mind-set of the Laodiceans, Christ called them to turn away from their business associates and seek Him. True riches do not reside in the culture around us.

The arrogant independence of the church is certainly the opposite of faith and repentance. The Laodicean church desperately needed to faithfully seek the face of God. "They are poor; but Christ has gold. They are naked; but Christ has clothes. They are blind; but Christ has eye salve. Let them no longer trust in their banks, their Phrygian eye powders and their clothing factories! Let them come to Him! He can enrich their poverty, clothe their nakedness, and heal their blindness ... He can enrich them with life and life abundant."[3]

Eternal riches cannot be purchased with a bank account. Isaiah said, "Come, everyone who is thirsty, come to the water; and you without silver, come, buy, and eat! Come, buy wine and milk without silver and without cost" (Isa. 55:1). If a church confesses its poverty, the riches of God are at its disposal. We do not buy from God through our goodness, determination, or with anything we have. God's coinage is confession of our poverty and need.

If we are conscious of our blindness, God has a cure and supplies spiritual illumination and understanding. This church that resided in a city known for its vision was informed that it was actually blind! They needed to come to the Lord and buy divine salve for their blindness if they wished to see.

What a shock their nakedness must have been to this church. Laodicea was famous for the clothing available there. The black sheep on the hillsides around Laodicea provided a plush wool that was sought after from all over the world. This self-sufficient congregation was unaware of its embarrassing nakedness.

If we are conscious of our nakedness, He has clothing for us. **White clothes** refers to the righteousness required to enter God's presence. To enter into His presence mandates that we be clothed in righteousness.

As many as I love, I rebuke and discipline. So be zealous and repent. If the Lord did not love the church, He would never have rebuked them. So, He directed them specifically to repent. The required cure was to be zealous for the Lord and repent. Everything depends on that. Without that response, Christ would vomit them out of His mouth. They were to repent immediately and continually practice the zeal of genuine faith in Christ.

The church needs to be set on fire for God. If my arm is numb and has no feeling, that is bad because pain is my friend. It tells me where the problem is. Indifference feels no pain and is unaware of any need. This lukewarm church had no concern for God. Their consciences were seared and their wills paralyzed. So the Lord called them to commitment and repentance.

Gracious Invitation (Rev. 3:20-21)

When we began these seven letters, Jesus was seen walking among the churches. He was with His people, in fellowship together with them. Now as these letters conclude, He has been excluded, He is outside the church. He is knocking to get back into the church. **See! I stand at the door and knock. If anyone hears my voice and opens the door, I will come in to him and eat with him, and he with me.** Laodicea did not see their need of Him anymore. They were rich and increased with material goods and were no longer needy.

Stand and *knock* are present tense verbs meaning that He continuously stands and knocks. Here we see the heart of the Savior. We see how much He longs to be in the midst of the church and among His people. The Lord knows that churches are made up of individuals. So He spoke now to just one individual—**anyone.** "Insulted, excluded, and ready to spew out of His mouth that which is utterly loathsome, He yet waits, knocking still at the door, willing to enter into new fellowship with one man."[4] If just one will hear His voice, He will come in. Coming back to the Lord has to be done one by one. Whoever opens the door will result in His coming in.

No doubt about it. No negotiations necessary. All that is required is to hear His voice and open the door, and He will come in. "The prospect of entering a home and dining with the family in the ancient Near East was the ultimate expression of human friendship, depicting the desire for an intimacy of relationship surpassed only by those relationships existing within an actual family. In this case the relationship involving the Lord may even be thought to exceed familial or filial relationships."[5]

To the one who conquers I will give the right to sit with me on my throne, just as I also conquered and sat down with my Father on his throne. If we welcome Him into our lives and churches, we will be associated with Him in His kingdom. His amazing grace now extended to those who conquered in the church at Laodicea, the magnificent privilege of sitting with Him on the throne of God. Grace is truly amazing!

This promise is given to believers with wholehearted devotion to the Lord, and it exceeds all the other promises found in these seven letters. The throne represents the very power and authority of God. It is offered to every believer, even the lukewarm believers in Laodicea. This brings us back to Revelation 1:6 where the Lord said that He has "made us a kingdom, priests to his God and Father—to him be glory and dominion forever and ever. Amen."

What a tragic ending to the letters to these strategic churches. We began with the Lord holding the pastors in His hands and walking among the churches. We end with Jesus standing on the outside knocking to get into His own church! Could it be that this is where we are today in America?

This is the tragic picture of many churches today. Enraptured in their own self-indulgence, oblivious to the reality of the spiritual power available to every believer, these churches are compromised and disobedient in the face of a world desperately needing the healing touch that can only come through faith in Jesus Christ.

Speaking of the challenges the church faces today in an increasingly hostile world, Os Guinness wrote, "The church that cannot say *no* to all that contradicts its Lord is a church that is well down the road to cultural defeat and captivity. But the courage to say *no* has to be followed by an equally clear, courageous and constructive *yes*—to the Lord Himself, to His gospel and His vision of life, humanity and the future, so that Christians can be seen to live differently and to live better in the world of today."[6] The world of the seven churches of Asia Minor has come to us today!

These strategic letters to seven churches are addressing the most crucial question of all: What is the relationship of Jesus Christ to the church? Is He joyfully received, adored, obeyed, praised, and honored? Or is He removed from intimacy with the church named for Himself, outside knocking for entrance?

A CLOSER LOOK

Laodicea

Taking advantage of being on a major road, Laodicea became one of the most important and successful cities in Asia Minor. The extreme prosperity created a strong interest in the Greek arts that supported the advancement of science and literature and the presence of a great medical school. The wealth of the city was vividly illustrated by the beautiful monuments of the city that were wondrously embellished.

The city minted its own coins, and inscriptions give evidence of the worship of Zeus, Asclepius, Apollo, and the emperors. From Rome it received the title of "free city" and was the chief city of the Roman Conventus, comprised of twenty-four additional cities. Cicero records that he held official Roman trials there about 50 BC.

The city ruins today give evidence of the presence of Roman luxury and extravagance. It became one of the most prosperous cities in all of Asia Minor.

Personal Reflection

1. Are your works hot, lukewarm, or cold? Explain.

2. How is it possible to say "I'm rich ... wealthy and need nothing" and not realize "you are wretched, pitiful, poor, blind, and naked" (v. 17)?

3. What does it mean to you that Jesus said, "As many as I love, I rebuke and discipline" (v. 19)?

1. Vance Havner, *Repent or Else* (New York: Fleming H. Revell, 1958) 81.
2. G. Campbell Morgan, *A First Century Message to Twentieth Century Christians* (New York: Fleming H. Revell, 1902) 215.
3. John Stott, *What Christ Thinks of the Church* (London: Angus Hudson Ltd., 1990) 121.
4. Morgan, 216.
5. Paige Patterson, *Revelation,* The New American Commentary, Volume 39 (Nashville: B&H, 2012) 144.
6. Os Guinness, *Impossible People* (Downer's Grove, IL: IVP Books, 2016) 22.